The Little Guidebook for Smart and Resourceful Boys

THE BOY'S BOOK OF ADVENTURE

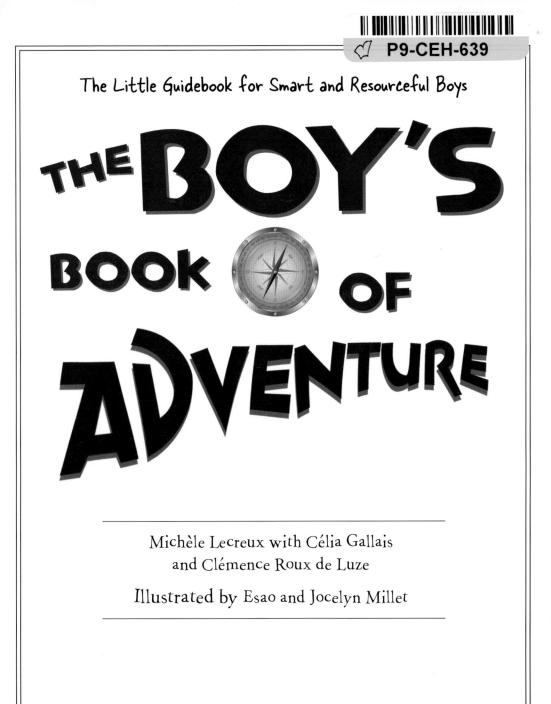

Michèle Lecreux with Célia Gallais
and Clémence Roux de Luze

Illustrated by Esao and Jocelyn Millet

 BARRON'S

Contents

Little Insects in the Grass.................................4

Bike Safety.................................8

Secret Codes.................................10

Make Your Own Wallet.................................14

Morse Code.................................16

Awalé.................................18

Protect Yourself from the Sun!.................................20

Wild Geometry.................................22

Trail Signs.................................25

Don't Lose North!.................................26

Rescue Techniques.................................30

Shells.................................32

Cool Drinks.................................34

The Outdoor Traveler's Toolbox.................................36

The Most Beautiful Rocks.................................38

The Adventurer's Shelter.................................40

Poisonous Snakes!.................................42

Make a Periscope.................................44

The Music of the Sea.................................48

First Aid.................................50

Taking Care of Plants Without
    Wasting Water.................................52

Reading a Map..54

Karate Sudoku...58

The Native American Way.....................................62

A Pond in Your Backyard......................................66

Make a Water Mill..70

The Music of the World...72

The Snail Race...76

What Will the Weather Be Like
      Tomorrow?..78

Your Head in the Stars...82

Races on the Water..86

Make an Herbarium..90

The Mystery of Cherries..94

The Adventurer's Pouch..95

How to Catch Fish..96

Bird-Watching..100

Sailors' Knots...104

Animal Tracks..108

A Garden...112

Send News!...116

The Martian...120

      Removing the Salt from Seawater..121

LITTLE INSECTS IN THE GRASS

Even an adventurer cannot know all the types of insects that live on Earth! Look at them.

★ BASIC PARTS OF INSECTS

☞ Insects all have a head, a thorax, and a stomach. The head has a pair of antennas, the thorax has a pair of legs and two pairs of wings, and the stomach has two pairs of legs!

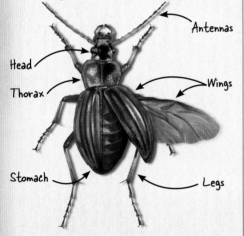

Head

Thorax

Antennas

Wings

Stomach

Legs

Sometimes insects appear to lack one pair of wings, but that's because the wings have changed shape. For example, the second pair of wings on a housefly has changed into flight controls.

Insects have no skeleton, but their bodies are covered with hard, solid shells. Some insects eat plants, others eat bugs that are smaller than they are, and others get their food by sucking the juice from plants or the blood from animals.

Insects lay eggs from which larvae hatch. The larvae change shape completely when they turn into adults. For example, butterflies lay eggs that give birth to little caterpillars. Later, their wings grow and they turn into butterflies.

DON'T BE CONFUSED

Spiders are not insects! They have eight legs and belong to the group called arachnids.

☞ MAYFLIES

Mayflies are tiny bugs that don't even have mouths for eating! It's true. They don't need one, for they live only a day or two in their adult forms. That gives them just enough time to lay eggs in pools of water!

☞ DRAGONFLIES

Dragonflies, with their bright colors and their helicopter shape, fly over swamps as they hunt. By moving their two pairs of wings, they can stay in one place as long as it takes to spot their prey. Do you know that dragonflies lived as early as the time of the dinosaurs, and that certain ones had a wingspan of 28 inches (70 cm)?

✳ PRAYING MANTISES

Even though praying mantises are very beautiful with their long bodies, they are fierce! They hang onto twigs to blend in with plants. Ready for an ambush, they remain still to surprise their prey. If they get the munchies, the females eat the males once the females' eggs are fertilized.

✳ BUTTERFLIES

Some butterflies have two black circles on their wings, which look like the eyes of a large animal. It is thought that the black circles serve to frighten away possible predators. Other butterflies change color throughout the year to look like the leaves around them!

GRASSHOPPERS, LOCUSTS, AND CRICKETS

Grasshoppers, locusts, and crickets are world champion long jumpers! By rubbing their long back legs against their wing cases (the rear wings), like a violin bow, they make "music." We say that they chirp. All these little bugs are real problems! Locusts travel in swarms and can destroy crops, especially in Africa.

ANTS

Ants, like bees, live in colonies around a single queen. But they are not satisfied to gather their food the way most insects do. Certain ants grow tiny mushrooms, and others raise herds of aphids (another kind of insect)!

In fact, aphids produce sweet-tasting liquid—a delicious treat for the ants and their larvae!

BEES

Bees live in a society called a swarm. At the head of each group of bees, there is a queen. Her role is to lay all the eggs for the colony! The others, the workers, take care of the larvae that come out of these eggs. The bees gather nectar from flowers and make honey to feed the larvae.

The scientists who study insects are called entomologists. Sometimes they need to watch the insects of a region. In order to capture the ones that come out only at night, without harming them, the entomologists stretch a large white sheet and shine a very powerful light onto it. Drawn by the light, the insects come and gather on the sheet in large numbers. You can have this experience some summer night, and you will be surprised at the number of different insects you will be able to watch.

BIKE SAFETY

Here's some advice before you jump onto your bike!

☞ KEEP YOUR BIKE IN SHAPE

You need to check a few things: Tires? Fully inflated! Brakes? OK!

Headlight? It works perfectly! At night, you must have light in front (yellow or white) and on the back (red).

If your bike doesn't have a headlight, you can get a light that attaches to the handlebars or around your lower leg or your arm.

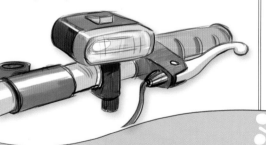

☞ USE THE RIGHT EQUIPMENT

Choose the right clothing. A vest with reflective stripes makes it easier to see you both day and night. If you ever have an accident, the most important thing to protect is your head. It's very important to wear a helmet!

The bell is used to alert other people. When you ride, you must be aware of what is going on around you. So don't put your hood up. And no MP3 player or cell phone! The music will keep you from hearing the sounds around you and the ones made by other users of the road.

☞ TRAFFIC RULES

Even on a country road, ride on the right side of the road, not in the middle! In a group, ride single file rather than side by side. That way the cars will be able to pass you safely.

Obey "Do Not Enter" signs and don't go the wrong way on a one-way road. To signal that you are going to turn, use your arm to point out the direction that you are going to take.

Do not stop suddenly without warning riders behind you. And be careful when braking with the front brake. You could end up flying over the handlebars!

ROAD SIGNS

Do you know them? Here are a few of them and what they mean:

STOP — Stop at a Stop Sign!

People Crossing

Bike Path

No Bicycles

Finally, if you stop for a break or walk away from your bike, use a bike lock.

You are ready for a two-wheel adventure!

SECRET CODES

Secret codes are necessary for swapping secrets! What adventurer does not have his own code?

❖ CHOOSE YOUR CODE! ❖

THERE ARE AN AMAZING NUMBER OF SECRET CODES. HERE ARE A FEW THAT YOU CAN USE.

☞ THE BACKWARD ALPHABET

The simplest of codes! Here is the alphabet in order, along with a backward alphabet.

Z = A	Q = J	H = S
Y = B	P = K	G = T
X = C	O = L	F = U
W = D	N = M	E = V
V = E	M = N	D = W
U = F	L = O	C = X
T = G	K = P	B = Y
S = H	J = Q	A = Z
R = I	I = R	

SECRET MESSAGE:
NVVG NV ZG GSV
LZP GIVV.

Answer: Meet me at the oak tree.

☞ THE LAWYER'S CODE

In this code, A is equal to K. Then the alphabet continues in order.

A = K	J = T	S = C
B = L	K = U	T = D
C = M	L = V	U = E
D = N	M = W	V = F
E = O	N = X	W = G
F = P	O = Y	X = H
G = Q	P = Z	Y = I
H = R	Q = A	Z = J
I = S	R = B	

SECRET MESSAGE:
S'VV GKSD PYB IYE KD DRO
MVOKBSXQ.

Answer: I'll wait for you at the clearing.

THE ROTTEN EGG CODE

In this code, E is used for I, then the alphabet continues in order.

A = W	E = A	I = E	M = I	Q = M	U = Q	Y = U
B = X	F = B	J = F	N = J	R = N	V = R	Z = V
C = Y	G = C	K = G	O = K	S = O	W = S	
D = Z	H = D	L = H	P = L	T = P	X = T	

SECRET MESSAGE: YKIA PK PDA YKPPWCA KJ PDA HWGA.

Answer: Come to the cottage on the lake.

JULIUS CAESAR'S CODE

We are told that Julius Caesar, the famous Roman Emperor, used this code to speak with his armies. A is equal to X.

A = X	G = D	M = J	S = P	Y = V
B = Y	H = E	N = K	T = Q	Z = W
C = Z	I = F	O = L	U = R	
D = A	J = G	P = M	V = S	
E = B	K = H	Q = N	W = T	
F = C	L = I	R = O	X = U	

SECRET MESSAGE: ALK'Q CLODBQ QEB MFZKFZ.

Answer: Don't forget the picnic.

THE ALPHABET IN NUMBERS

The code where the letters are replaced by numbers is trickier. It produces even stranger messages that are difficult to decode.

1 = A	5 = E	9 = I	13 = M	17 = Q	21 = U	25 = Y
2 = B	6 = F	10 = J	14 = N	18 = R	22 = V	26 = Z
3 = C	7 = G	11 = K	15 = O	19 = S	23 = W	
4 = D	8 = H	12 = L	16 = P	20 = T	24 = X	

SECRET MESSAGE: 3 1 12 12 13 5.

Answer: Call me.

THE DECODING DISK

This will serve you well in making up codes that nobody will ever be able to decode, except for your best friend!

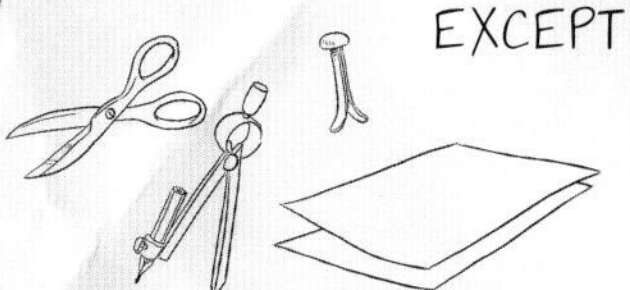

1 Cut out two cardboard circles, one slightly larger than the other.

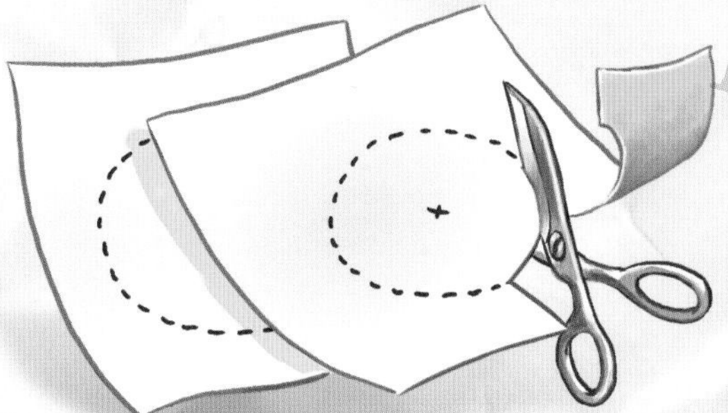

MATERIALS:
- THICK PAPER
- 1 PAPER FASTENER
- A DRAWING COMPASS
- A PAIR OF SCISSORS

2 Poke a hole in the center and put the two circles together using a paper fastener (with the head facing up).

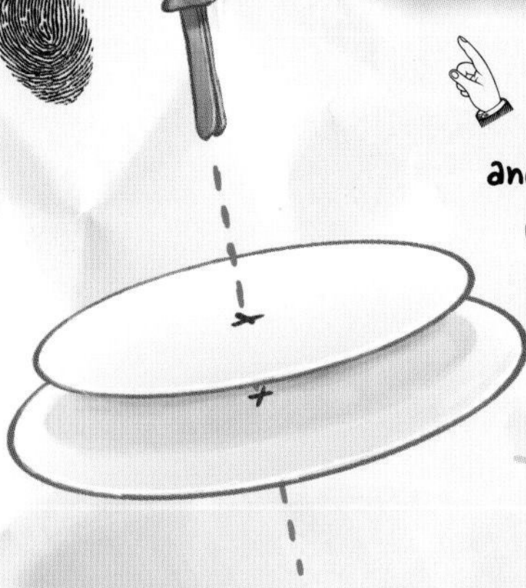

3 Write the letters of the alphabet clockwise around the edge of the larger circle.

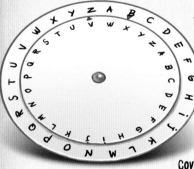

☝ 4 Then write the letters of the alphabet around the edge of the smaller circle, opposite the ones on the larger circle.

Now you will be able to code and decode messages easily! For example, to write in the lawyer's code, turn the smaller circle so that K lines up with the A on the larger outer circle. Look at how the letters line up. Now all you have to do is write your secret message!

HOW TO DECODE

If you create a new code, what do you do so that your friend can decode it? It's simple: Mark a little triangle in pencil above one letter on the top circle and under another one on the bottom circle that are lined up (it doesn't matter which letters).

Turn the smaller circle to the left or the right to choose the positioning of the letters in your new code.

Careful! At the start of your text, note the direction and the number of the letters separating the two triangles! For example, "left, + 2." Once you have written the message, cover your trail to keep outsiders away: Turn the disk so that it doesn't match anything! But give your friend the decoding instructions. By lining up the two triangles, he will know that he has to go in the opposite direction, or "right, - 2" to find the code!

But shhh! It's a secret.

MAKE YOUR OWN WALLET

EVEN WHEN YOU ARE NOT OFF ON AN ADVENTURE, YOU ALWAYS HAVE PAPERS AND A LITTLE MONEY TO CARRY. A SMALL WALLET IS VERY HANDY FOR KEEPING EVERYTHING IN ORDER.

MATERIALS

- A BIG SHEET OF THICK PAPER, 10 × 26 INCHES (25 × 65 CM) (OR A LARGE PIECE OF POSTER BOARD)
- A PAIR OF SCISSORS

1 Fold the sheet of paper in half the long way, then make a fold 3/4 of an inch (2 cm) from each edge.

2 Then make two folds to divide the rest of the surface into three equal parts. Put the paper down flat again.

A	B	C	D	E	F	G	H

3 Now follow the model and make "valley" folds (downward folds) along the green lines, and "mountain" folds (upward folds) along the red ones.

D	C	B	A

4 Fold in two on the middle fold (between D and E).

5 Now fold the little flap A onto part B.

D	C	B	A

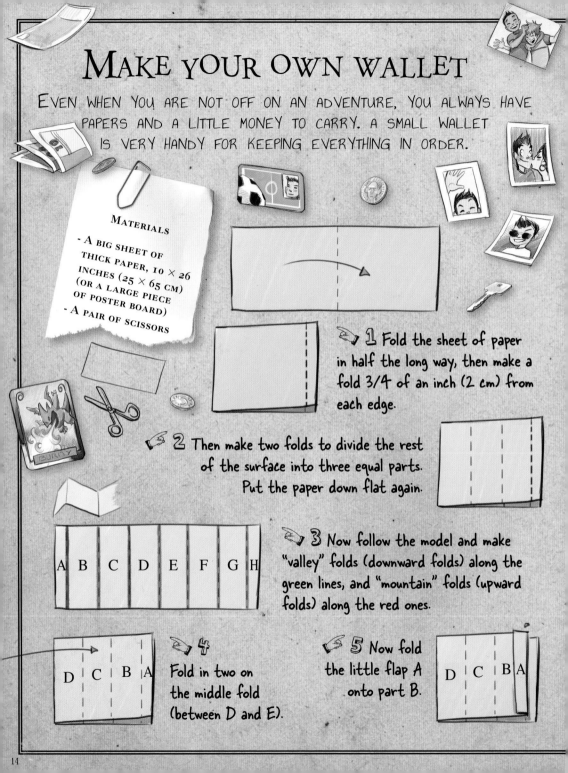

14

6 Fold part C back onto part D.

7 Close part G–H onto F–A.

8 Fold the little flap H inside the fold so that it covers little flap A.

9 Fold the whole thing in two by folding B onto G.

10 Fold the whole thing in two the long way.

11 Cut off two corners.

12 Now, on each side of the wallet, you have six tabs. Slide your hand between three and four, fold together three tabs from each side, and tuck them into this opening. Do the same thing on the other side and you are done!

You have a very useful wallet that has two pockets with openings on the top, and two other pockets with openings along the sides. You can use it to hold money, papers, photos—everything that an adventurer needs to carry!

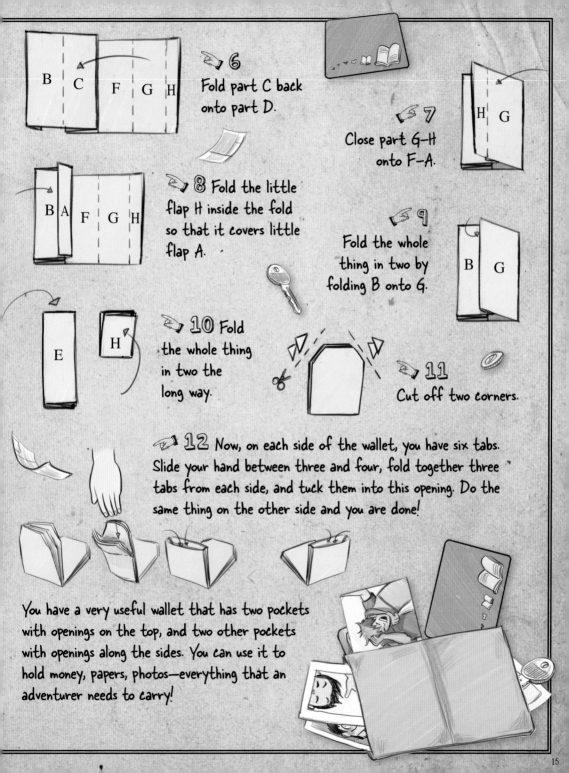

MORSE CODE

This code was invented in the nineteenth century by Samuel Morse.

☞ DOTS AND DASHES...

In Morse code, every letter of the alphabet is replaced by dashes and/or dots.

☞ TIMING...

Stick to this timing: One dash lasts as long as three dots; the space between two letters lasts as long as three dots; and the space between two words lasts as long as seven dots.

You can choose how long a dot lasts! At night, to "speak" in the dark, use Morse code with light signals! Turn on a flashlight briefly to make the dots, and for a longer time to make the dashes.

☞ ...MEMORY

It's best when you know Morse code by heart. Learn the easiest letters, the ones that have only dots: E I S H, and the ones that have only dashes: T M O. Then learn the letters that have both dots and dashes (see the chart below).

Dots Only		
E : .		
I : ..		
S : ...		
H :		

	O : _ _ _		

	2 dots and dashes		
	A : . _		
	N : _ .		

Dashes Only	3 dots and dashes		
T : _	D : _ ..		
M : _ _	G : _ _ .		

	K : _ . _		
	R : . _ .		
	U : .. _		
	W : . _ _		

4 dots and dashes		
B : _ ...		
C : _ . _ .		
F : .. _ .		

J : . _ _ _		
L : . _ ..		
P : . _ _ .		
Q : _ _ . _		
V : ... _		
X : _ .. _		
Y : _ . _ _		
Z : _ _ ..		

☞ THE MOST FAMOUS MESSAGE: SOS

Three short taps, three long taps, three short taps. Someone is calling for help! All rescuers in the world know this signal of distress. This message must be sent without a space between the letters!

✖ AN ALL-TERRAIN TELEPHONE ✖

MORSE CODE WAS CREATED FOR THE TELEGRAPH, THE ANCESTOR OF THE TELEPHONE.

MATERIALS:
- 2 TIN CANS (OR SODA CANS), EMPTIED AND WASHED
- A STRING ABOUT 6 FEET (2 M) LONG
- A SMALL HAMMER
- A NAIL OR A SCREWDRIVER

☞ 1 Ask an adult to remove the tops of the cans; then using the hammer, flatten the sharp edges.

☞ 2 Ask the adult to poke a hole in the center of the bottom of each can.

☞ 3 Thread the ends of the string into the cans from the outside.

☞ 4 Tie a knot in each end of the string.

☞ 5 Hold one of the cans in front of your mouth. Have a friend take the other can and hold it to his ear.

To send your message in Morse code, clearly say a short "dit" for each dot and a long "daaah" for each dash. Now have fun!

GOOD ADVICE

NOTE: IN ORDER FOR THE SOUND TO BE SENT WELL, THE STRING BETWEEN THE TWO CANS NEEDS TO BE PULLED VERY TIGHT.

AWALÉ

Awalé is a very well-known board game in Africa. Depending on the region, it has different names, but the way it is played is the same.

Awalé involves a board with twelve holes and forty-eight game pieces.

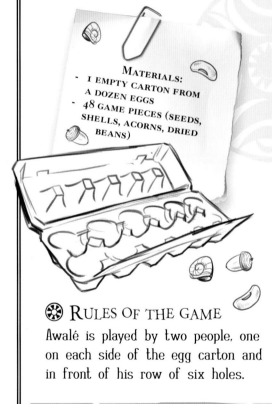

MATERIALS:
- 1 EMPTY CARTON FROM A DOZEN EGGS
- 48 GAME PIECES (SEEDS, SHELLS, ACORNS, DRIED BEANS)

✸ RULES OF THE GAME

Awalé is played by two people, one on each side of the egg carton and in front of his row of six holes.

Each player puts four seeds or other game pieces into each hole. Now the game can begin!

The first player chooses one of his holes and takes all the seeds out of it. Then he spreads them in a counterclockwise direction by putting the first seed into the hole located immediately to the right of the one where he removed the four seeds. The second seed goes into the following hole, and so forth.

The player continues placing the seeds in his hand one by one, whether into his own holes or those of the other side, without skipping any holes, and always moving in the same direction.

When the player has placed all his seeds, he can **remove some more, under two conditions:**
- The last hole where he placed a seed is a **hole belonging to the other player;**
- and, in this last hole, there are **two or three seeds**, neither more nor less.

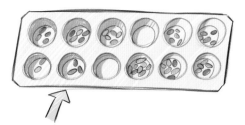

If the two conditions are met, the player takes the two or three seeds, removes them from the game, and places them in front of him. Then he looks into the next hole, that is the one located just to the left of the hole that he has just emptied. Are the same two conditions met here too? If so, the rule applies again! When the player has taken

all possible seeds, his turn is over. Now it's the other player's turn to place and remove, if he can.

☛ Forbidden Moves
Awalé is a game for two players. You are not allowed to leave the other player's holes empty—in other words, to "starve" the other player! You have to "feed him." So if a player is at risk of losing all his seeds, the other player makes a move to provide at least one seed to him.

☛ Game Over!
When one player's holes are empty and the other player no longer has enough seeds to "feed him," the game stops. The players count the seeds removed and the one who has the most wins.

PROTECT YOURSELF FROM THE SUN!

In the summer, even adventurers protect themselves from heat and sunburn!

Good Advice

Put on sunscreen at least every two hours, because by this time the skin sucks up all the lotion.

The number written on the bottle tells you the level of protection from the sun. Chose an index of at least fifty, because the higher the index, the better the protection for your skin.

But it all depends on what your skin is like! So you need to understand that light skin is more sensitive to the sun than dark skin.

Careful:
There is no such thing as a total sunscreen!

Our skin is very sensitive to the sun's ultraviolet (UV) rays. Staying in the sun for a long time without protection can lead to burns and other harm to the body. So here are some precautions to take:

☞ The sun is most dangerous when it's highest in the sky, between noon and 4:00 in the afternoon. If you plan to go out, leave early in the morning to take advantage of the cool hours.

☞ During the lunch hour, stay in the shade, avoid physical exercise, and keep your T-shirt and cap on.

☞ To protect your eyes, there is nothing better than a good pair of sunglasses.

★ THE DESERT SCARF ★

The Touareg people live in the desert. They would never think of walking around with their heads uncovered. They use a special long scarf rolled around their heads. You, too, can learn how to tie it!

1 ☞ Place a large scarf at least 6 feet (2 m) long on top of your head and bring the two ends together in front of you.

2 ☞ Twist this piece of fabric around itself all the way up to your forehead (as if you were drying it out).

3 ☞ Then wrap it around your head several times.

Now you are all set—no more risk of sunstroke.

4 ☞ Next, tuck the end under one of the coils you have just made.

☞ If you also want to protect your face during a sandstorm, the scarf has to be at least 12 feet (4 m) long.

1 Place the scarf on your head and let 3 feet (1 m) of it hang down onto one shoulder. Bring one length in front of you and twist it around.

2 Wrap this twisted part around your head several times.

3 Take the length touching your shoulder and spread it across your face. Tuck the end between the coils of fabric.

WILD GEOMETRY

At school, you have instruments
for measuring things, but in nature,
adventurers get by without them!
They know the old ways.

◉ MEASURING WITH YOUR BODY ◉

Today we measure things in inches, centimeters, and meters. Long ago, people used their bodies. Here are some ancient units of measure.

⌁ THE FOOT
the length of a large foot

⌁ THE CUBIT
with the arm bent at a right angle, this is the length from the elbow to the tip of the middle finger, approximately 17½ inches (44 cm)

⌁ THE HAND SPAN
the distance between the tip of the thumb and the tip of the little finger with the hand spread wide, approximately 9 inches (23 cm)

0 1 2 3 4 5 6 7 8 9 10 11 12 13 14 15 16 17 18 19 20 21 22

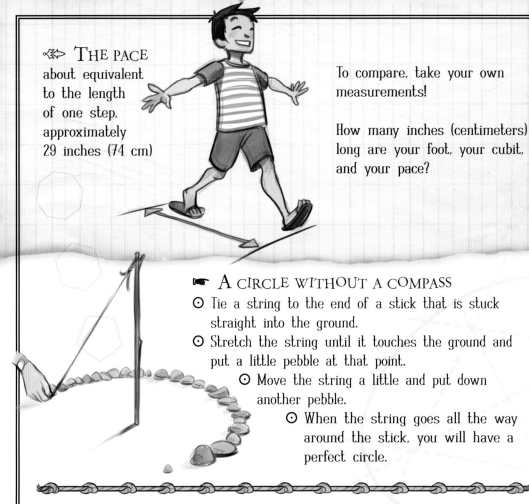

THE PACE

about equivalent to the length of one step, approximately 29 inches (74 cm)

To compare, take your own measurements!

How many inches (centimeters) long are your foot, your cubit, and your pace?

A CIRCLE WITHOUT A COMPASS

⊙ Tie a string to the end of a stick that is stuck straight into the ground.

⊙ Stretch the string until it touches the ground and put a little pebble at that point.

⊙ Move the string a little and put down another pebble.

⊙ When the string goes all the way around the stick, you will have a perfect circle.

RIGHT ANGLE WITHOUT A SQUARE

During the Middle Ages, architects built cathedrals using a cord with thirteen knots.

◣ Just as they did, make thirteen knots spaced out evenly on a string about 6 feet (2 m) long.

◣ Make a triangle on a flat surface: The shortest side has four knots; the second side has five; and the last one has six. Do you see the right angle?

☞ USING THE SUN TO MEASURE HEIGHT

If you want to measure a tall tree or a house, all you need to know is the length of its shadow! A scientist in ancient times, Thales, used this technique to measure the height of the pyramids of Egypt!

Height of the tree =
$$\frac{\text{length of the shadow of the tree}}{\text{length of the shadow of the stick}}$$

→ On a sunny day, poke a large stick into the ground near the tree you want to measure. The part that sticks above the ground must be exactly 3 feet (1 m).

→ Measure the shadow of the stick in paces or feet. Then measure the length of the tree's shadow in the same way. If, for example, the shadow of the stick 3 feet (1 m) tall measures 2 feet (60 cm), and the shadow of the tree measures 10 feet (300 cm), you know that the tree is five times taller than your stick.

So it is
15 feet (4.5 m) high!

TRAIL SIGNS

*Adventurers leave strange
signs in the woods.
Do you know what they mean?*

To follow a trail or to create one, an adventurer needs to know what the signs that other people have left in the wild before him mean.

He must also be capable of leaving them himself with whatever he has to work with, such as soil, sand, pebbles, or branches.

HERE ARE THE MAIN TRAIL SIGNS:

Follow this direction, I went this way.

There is a hidden message three paces in this direction.

Watch out: obstacle to cross

Hurry!

This is a false trail!

I went home.

Stay here; don't move!

DON'T LOSE NORTH!

To become an adventurer who is worthy of the title, learn to get your bearings without a compass and a map.

★ DURING THE DAY ☾

☞ You know that the sun rises in the east and sets in the west, so the shadows that it casts are headed toward the west in the morning and toward the east in the evening. In the middle of the day, the sun is at its highest point, right above you. Then your shadow is smaller in size. In order to find north in the morning and the afternoon, all you have to do is to poke a stick about 12 inches (30 cm) long into the ground in an open area. Put a pebble at the end of the shadow cast by the stick. Wait at least an hour and then mark the new location of the end of the shadow with a second pebble.

Draw a line on the ground between the two pebbles. You know that it is oriented east-west. Your stick is to the south of the line, and north is exactly opposite, on the other side of the line!

South is located on the perpendicular of this line, on the side of the stick.

North is located opposite south.

What DOESN'T WORK

People say that all you have to do is look at the side of trees where moss grows in order to locate north. This is false! Moss grows on the coolest and most humid side of trees, and that is not always north.

★ ON A DARK NIGHT ☾

AT NIGHT, THERE ARE SOME VERY USEFUL REFERENCE POINTS TO HELP YOU GET YOUR BEARINGS: STARS! IN ANCIENT TIMES, SEAMEN USED THEM TO FIND THEIR WAY AT SEA.

🖝 If you are in the **Northern Hemisphere** of our planet (in North America, for example), it's easy. You just have to know a few stars to find your bearings. The North Star, which always shows north, is part of the constellation Ursa Minor. It is very bright, but not always easy to locate at first glance! There is a very simple way to find it, however.

Place yourself in a good open area away from lights and look upward. Among the thousands of stars, find the constellation the Big Dipper, which gets its name from its shape, and is also known as Ursa Major. Then imagine a line that extends the outer edge of the "dipper" and is five times as long. This leads you directly to a very bright star, the North Star! It is at the end of the tail of the Little Bear, Ursa Minor.

Earth's North Pole is always in the direction of this star.

🖝 If you are in the **Southern Hemisphere**, you discover that the sky has different stars (of course, we don't see the same stars from one hemisphere to the other). There is no Big Dipper, but there is Centaurus (a constellation in the shape of a half man, half horse), below which you need to look for a cluster of four stars that form a diamond (like a kite-shape). This is the Southern Cross.

Earth's South Pole is located in the direction of the large branch of the Southern Cross.

NOW IT'S IMPOSSIBLE TO LOSE NORTH!

Make a
❋ FLOATING COMPASS ❋

MATERIALS

- 1 CORK (OR 1 SMALL PIECE OF PACKING FOAM)
- 1 SEWING NEEDLE
- 1 PERMANENT MARKER
- 1 PLASTIC BOTTLE
- A MAGNET
- A KNIFE

1 ☞

Ask an adult to cut the bottle off around 4 inches (10 cm) from the bottom. Fill the bottom with water. Ask an adult to cut a round slice off the cork.

☞ 2

With the permanent marker draw the cardinal points of the compass, as in the illustration.

3 ☞

Rub the pointed end of the needle across the magnet several times, always in the same direction.

4 ☞ Stick the magnetized needle into the round slice of cork, entering at the point indicating south. Make it stick out the north side.

5 ☞ Carefully place this on the surface of the water. Turn the circular disc around and then let it go.

6 ☞

The magnetized needle always ends up pointing north, like the little Chinese fish that indicated the south with its head and north with its tail!

GOOD ADVICE

YOU WILL HAVE TO RUB YOUR NEEDLE ON THE MAGNET REGULARLY, BECAUSE IT LOSES ITS MAGNETISM QUICKLY.

☞ THE CHINESE COMPASS

In a very ancient Chinese book, dating from the year 1040, there is a description of a "fish that looks south." The book explains that this "fish" was very useful in keeping from getting lost, especially for seamen. The little fish was made from a very thin sheet of magnetized metal. It was placed on the water, which helped its movements toward the south, according to the direction taken by the ship. Do you know that Europe "invented" the compass five hundred years later?

S   N

RESCUE TECHNIQUES

Sometimes even the most careful adventurer takes a fall and gets hurt; so it's a good idea to know a couple of rescue techniques.

☞ A HAND CHAIR

If a friend twists his ankle, he should not put any weight on it. You just need two people to carry him.

☞ CAREFUL

You should never act as a rescue worker. It can be very dangerous to move an injured person! The best thing to do is to alert an adult, who will call a doctor. But if one of your buddies falls and is conscious, you can still help him get to a place where he can get treatment.

Facing each other, two rescuers grab their own left wrists with their right hands. Then they grab their left hand onto the right wrist of the other rescuer. The hands then form a type of seat. The injured person can sit on it and lean on the shoulders of his rescuers.

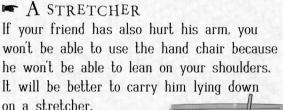

EEE-E-E-EE!

☞ A STRETCHER

If your friend has also hurt his arm, you won't be able to use the hand chair because he won't be able to lean on your shoulders. It will be better to carry him lying down on a stretcher.

→ Place a blanket flat on the ground.
→ Find two long poles of strong wood: brooms, rakes, or skis if there is snow.
→ Put one pole a third of the way in from the edge of the blanket.
→ Fold the third of the cloth over the pole.

→ Put the other pole onto the first third of this folded cloth.
→ Then fold the rest of the cloth over the two poles.

When the injured person lies down on the stretcher, his weight holds the folds in place.

☞ A BANDAGE

Have you hurt your hand in a fall? Here's how to make a bandage with a scarf.

1 Fold your scarf in two to produce a long band.

2 Pull the scarf between your thumb and the palm of your hand.

3 Cross the two lengths on the back of your hand, and then again on your wrist.

4 Make a knot around your wrist with the two ends of the scarf.

SHELLS

It's not always easy to put a name to a shell. Here's something to help you figure them out.

☞ SOFT-SHELL CLAM
The color of the soft-shell clam is grayish, and the shape is more elongated than that of the cockle clam. It, too, lives in the muddy and sandy bottoms.

☞ RAZOR CLAM
A razor clam is long, rectangular, and brown. It lives deeper down. You have to sprinkle some salt on the two holes that it makes in the surface, and up it comes! Now you have to grab it.

☞ COCKLE CLAM
Cupped and grooved, the shell of the cockle clam is light in color and thick. You will find lots of these, empty, on the beach near the water. The cockle clam is gathered at low tide. It lives in the mud near the surface, and it can be spotted by the two little holes close together that it makes in the mud. You can dig it up easily with a spoon or a rake. You can also stamp on the mud to make it come to the surface.

☞ SPOTTED COWRIE
The spotted cowrie measures only 3/8 of an inch (1 cm) and is found among the rocks in the gravel. It has a pink or purplish color with small spots and little grooves.

FILE YOLDIA

The file yoldia is larger and rounder than the cockle clam. You will recognize it by the color of the white shell mixed with brown.

DONAX

Donax are small and long. They are pretty, with grooved shells and shades of beige.

LIMPET

A limpet's shell is another one that has a cone shape. The limpet lives on rocks. There are several types of limpets. The shell looks a little like plaid!

ABALONE

The abalone lives on rocks not far from the surface of the water. Because of its round, long shape and the mother-of-pearl inside it, it is sometimes also known as the ear shell.

SPIRAL SHELLS

WHELK

The whelk is an edible mollusk that you may have eaten. The thick shell forms a spiral and measures between 2½-4 inches (6-10 cm). You will see it only in a spring tide.

TURITELLE

The turitelle has a very small pointed spiral shell. It's hard to find this shell whole; it is often broken.

PERIWINKLE

Periwinkle is a pretty name for this tiny shell, 3/8 of an inch (1 cm), which looks like a snail's shell. It lives by eating certain types of algae.

COOL DRINKS

Every adventurer carries a canteen, but how do you get a cool drink in the middle of the summer?

☞ THE EGYPTIAN COOLER

The ancient Egyptians used this technique. You need a large, unglazed clay flowerpot. Plug the hole in the bottom of the pot with gravel or soil. Fill the pot with water, put your canteen into it, and cover it all with a dish towel. Leave the pot in the bright sun! The water slowly passes through the clay of the pot (and this is why it must be unglazed!) and evaporates because it is heated by the sun.

This evaporation produces coolness. The water contained in the pot does not heat up.

☞ A PORTABLE COOLER

If you go for a hike, the night before prepare a large plastic bottle. Fill it three-quarters full of water and put it into the freezer overnight.

The next day put this bottle in the center of your backpack. The sun will slowly heat the ice, but before it melts entirely it will keep your noon picnic cool! Once the ice melts, you can drink the water!

NATURAL COOLERS

If you have a picnic on the bank of a river, sink your canteen in the water, along with your whole picnic!

 Careful! Place everything into a large waterproof bag. Using a string, tie it to a small, low branch so you don't watch it get swept away by the current!

Also, if you are at the beach, put your snack and canteen into a plastic bag. Dig a hole in the sand and bury your bag with the handles sticking out. You will find everything nice and cool when you are hungry or thirsty!

CHOOSE YOUR MENU CAREFULLY

Don't bring foods that spoil easily. A banana quickly turns black, ham quickly changes color with heat (smoked ham is a better choice), milk sours. Tomatoes, cucumbers, hard-boiled eggs, bread, and sausage stay much fresher. A pasta salad with raisins keeps very well, and will also give you lots of energy!

When you stop for a little break, remember to put your backpack in the shade of a tree rather than leaving it in the sun.

THE OUTDOOR TRAVELER'S TOOLBOX

Are you heading out for a hike? Here are some very useful clothing ideas.

BACKPACK

Remember to put the heaviest things into the large pocket in the bag. Divide the binoculars, flashlight, magnifying glass, and other items among the outer pockets where you can get them more easily.

SHOES

They are very important, because you are going to be walking for a long time. Forget flip-flops and sandals—save them for the beach! Choose a good pair of sneakers or, better yet, some light, comfortable hiking boots that support your ankles. One bit of good advice: If the boots are new, wear them some before your outing; blisters are a hiker's enemy.

CLOTHING

Your clothing must be light and comfortable. Avoid tight jeans that will restrict your movements and choose natural materials such as cotton or linen. In the woods, long pants are a better choice than shorts, to avoid scratches from branches and thorns. Ideally, you should wear three layers: an undershirt (or T-shirt), a sweatshirt (or fleece) to keep you warm, and a windbreaker in case of bad weather.

☛ ACCESSORIES

Don't forget your sunglasses and your cap or a hat. A scarf is also very useful. Worn around your neck, it protects the back of your neck from sunburn; on your head, it replaces your cap if you have lost it, and it can even be turned into an emergency backpack!

HOW TO MAKE AN EMERGENCY BACKPACK

In Japan, this traditional method of folding is called furoshiki.

MATERIALS
2 LARGE SQUARE SCARVES, OR 1 VERY LARGE SQUARE SCARF
1 PIECE OF ROPE ABOUT 3 FEET (1 M) LONG

☛ **1** If you don't have any rope, roll up the first scarf to produce a long, thin strap.

2 ☛ Fold the second scarf diagonally to form a triangle.

☛ **3** Tie together the two tips at the top of the triangle.

4 ☛ Spread the two thicknesses of cloth and slide in the rope or the rolled scarf. Center the rope below the knot.

☛ **5** Tie the ends of the rope to the points of the cloth triangle.

There you have it: The rope or the rolled scarf forms the straps of your emergency backpack!

THE MOST BEAUTIFUL ROCKS

You can discover all kinds of rocks on a hike. What are their names and histories?

ROCKS ARE CLASSIFIED IN THREE LARGE FAMILIES.

1 ROCKS THAT CAME FROM VOLCANOES

Igneous rocks came from the lava of volcanoes. In contact with air or water, the lava cooled quickly. The rocks did not crystallize totally. In that case, basalt is formed—a black or gray stone. If the rocks that came from the magma (hot liquid rocks) took thousands of years to cool and harden, they formed granite, which is pink, gray, or white, with minerals visible to the naked eye.

2 ROCKS THAT FORMED AT THE BOTTOM OF THE SEA

Sedimentary rocks were formed through the pile up of all kinds of debris, such as pieces of rocks, shells, or animal remains. Limestone and clay are two examples, along with sandstone, which was formed by countless grains of sand stuck together.

3 ROCKS THAT WERE TRANSFORMED

Metamorphic rocks such as marble, slate, and schist are rocks that were already formed but were swallowed up in the earth at high temperatures and put under high pressure.

☞ ROUND ROCKS?

Round rocks are large boulders. Little by little, erosion from rain made them break. Pieces fell into rivers, where they got carried downstream by the water and worn away. That's why pebbles are round!

☞ FLOATING ROCKS?

These are lava rocks. When they are shot out by volcanoes, they fly through the air very violently, and they cool quickly and trap air bubbles. This is why they are so light and float!

☞ WONDERFUL GEODES

These types of grayish balls hide beautiful treasures inside. When the lava comes out of a volcano, it cools immediately: The surface hardens. Inside, a chemical change takes place, and multicolored crystals form!

☞ ROCKS THAT GROW

Stalactites and stalagmites form in caves. Rainwater travels through the limestone rock and dissolves it. Then, drop by drop, the water falls and leaves a limestone deposit at the tip of the stalactites—and on the ground, forming a stalagmite! One trick to remember the difference between the two: Remember that a stalactite has to hold tight so it doesn't fall off the ceiling of the cave!

THE ADVENTURER'S SHELTER

Build an adventurer's shelter at the back of your yard or in the middle of the forest.

☞ THE IDEAL SHELTER

Your shelter needs to be solid so it doesn't blow down at the first gust of wind, and large enough to invite a friend in. It also has to be simple so it doesn't frighten the animals and harm the scenic beauty. Make sure you don't damage any trees by cutting branches. It's far better to pick up branches that have fallen to the ground.

☞ FRAMEWORK

Find a tree with a fork higher than 3 feet (1 m). Collect some leafless branches about 5 feet (1.5 m) long. One of these branches must be the same height as the tree fork and must also be forked. Stick it firmly into the ground. Place the longest branch horizontally between the two forks.

Then place some wood poles at an angle on both sides of your shelter.

☞ COVER YOUR SHELTER

Find what you need to cover your shelter. It will look different based on what you find. Branches with leaves will make your shelter look like a bush.

☞ A SHELTER YOU CAN TAKE APART

The Native Americans of the Great Plains made their tipis with long wooden poles covered with bison hide. To change camps, they took everything apart and took the poles. That way they could put their tipis back together in a different place. You can adopt the same technique! Keep the poles from the structure of your shelter so you can build it again on your next vacation.

It's the ideal den for watching the forest animals.

If you use dead branches, your shelter will be more noticeable, but sturdier.

So you have only a few branches and the "walls" of your shelter are not filled in? Don't worry, there is always an answer. Put a large plastic tarp over the shelter that you have built and cover it with soil and grass.

POISONOUS SNAKES!

Some snakes are poisonous and others are not. Do you know the difference?

Only poisonous snakes are dangerous. Fortunately, you can buy snakebite kits. An adventurer who heads into an area where there are poisonous snakes should always have a snakebite kit with him!

☞ **POISONOUS OR HARMLESS?**

POISONOUS	HARMLESS

Head

Triangular, covered with small scales

Oval, with larger scales

Eyes

The pupil forms a vertical line.

The pupil is round.

Size

Generally smaller than harmless snakes

About 28 inches (70 cm) long

☞ DANGER — POISON!

A poisonous snake has venom glands connected to the fangs in its mouth. When it bites, it injects its venom.

☞ KEEP AWAY FROM POISONOUS SNAKES

Generally, poisonous snakes attack while hunting or if they feel threatened. Are you in a risky spot? Then put on long pants and high-topped boots. Don't put your hands among the rocks where snakes hide. Stomp with your feet or strike the ground with a stick: Snakes will feel the vibrations, and they will go away.

☞ HAVE YOU BEEN BITTEN?

Don't panic! Call a doctor, lie down, and stay calm. Do not suck on the wound! The place where you got bitten must be kept lower than the level of your heart. A snakebite is rarely fatal, but it may make you dizzy or make you feel like throwing up.

Types of POISONOUS SNAKES

✳ The rattlesnake likes rocky, dry areas and the heat. It is found mainly in the southern and western parts of the U.S.

✳ The copperhead, which can grow even longer than the rattlesnake, lives in the east and southeast and as far west as eastern Oklahoma and Texas.

Snake SKIN

✳ In order to grow larger, snakes lose their skins all at once; underneath, there is a bigger and longer skin. This is known as shedding. You can find pieces of snake skin in the wild. A snake's skin is nearly transparent.

Make a
PERISCOPE

Useful for seeing—without being seen!

The periscope is an instrument used by submarines for looking above the surface of the water when they are underneath it. But adventurers know how to use a periscope in many other instances—for example, when watching a bird's nest while remaining hidden behind a bush.

Materials
- 2 EMPTY MILK OR FRUIT JUICE CARTONS
- 2 SMALL MIRRORS ABOUT 2¾ INCHES × 4 INCHES (7 × 10 CM)
- 1 PAIR OF SCISSORS
- 1 PROTRACTOR
- 1 PENCIL

1 👉 It's easy to find small mirrors in stores. If your mother or older sister has some mirrors in her purse, ask permission before taking them!

2

Cut off the top of one container and carefully wash the inside, because often there is still some milk or fruit juice at the bottom.

3

Cut out a 2-inch (5-cm) square from one of the sides of the container. Be sure to leave 3/4 of an inch (2 cm) of cardboard all around the square.

4 Now you have to carefully position the first mirror: lay the carton down and cut a slit on the side next to the one where you made a window. Careful! This slit must be positioned very precisely.

If you have a protractor, measure a 45-degree angle starting at the angle closest to the bottom of the window. Draw it onto the carton before carefully cutting it.

GOOD ADVICE

IF YOU DON'T HAVE A PROTRACTOR, TAKE A LITTLE SQUARE OF CARDBOARD AND FOLD IT IN TWO ALONG THE DIAGONAL; THIS MAKES A MODEL FOR A 45-DEGREE ANGLE.

45°

5

The slit you just cut must be of a size and thickness so you can slide in the first mirror with the mirror surface facing up.

6

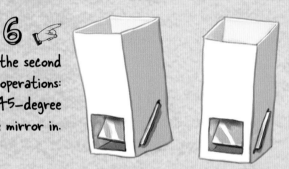

Take the second carton and the second mirror. Repeat the last operations: Cut the window, make a 45-degree slit, and slide the mirror in.

7

Now all you have to do is slide one carton into the other one as shown.

The window cut into the lower container faces you. The window cut into the upper container is on the other side.

👉 8

To make your periscope good and solid, tape the two cartons together.

👉 9

Hide behind a wall or a bush and bring the periscope up to your eyes. You can watch everything that's reflected in the upper mirror!

This is ideal for secretly watching shy little birds that fly away when people come near.

THE MUSIC OF THE SEA

Do you know that you can make sounds with seashells and even play music?

☛ TAHITIAN CONCHES
Conches are large shells. The Tahitians (Pacific islanders) use them as musical instruments! You may not find such large shells on the beach where you go for vacation; but if you find one in a spiral shape with a hole in the end, you can turn it into a whistle.

☛ THE SOUND OF THE WAVES
You can hear the sound of the waves in a spiral-shaped shell without a hole in it. Place it over your ear and listen carefully.

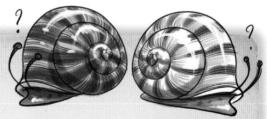

☛ THE RIGHT DIRECTION
When shells are shaped like spirals, nearly all of them in the world coil in a clockwise direction.
Scientists cannot explain the reason for this, but they have noted that very few shells are coiled in the other direction. The latter are so rare that they have been given special names: *Pyrolofusus deformis* (having a strange shape, in Latin), *Busycon contrarium* (contrary, in Latin), and *Triphoa perversa* (unusual, in Latin).

A MOBILE THAT CLANRS

MATERIALS
- Some shells with holes in them
- Some string
- Some sticks

☞ **1** Carefully save all the types of shells with holes in them that you find. When you have enough shells, tie pieces of string of different lengths onto them (one string per shell).

☞ **2** Set aside the longest stick. Tie the strings attached to the shells to the sticks (several strings per stick).

☞ **3** Cut as many new pieces of string as there are sticks. Now attach the ends of the strings to the middle of each stick.

☞ **4** Tie each other end of the strings at regular spaces to the biggest of the sticks.

☞ **5** Hang your mobile in a place where the wind blows. It will move at the slightest breeze, and you will hear the shells clank as they hit each other.

FIRST AID

Do you have a little boo-boo? As a careful adventurer, you can learn to take care of small injuries.

STINGS

Many insects sting only when they are threatened. If a wasp circles your picnic, stay calm and don't try to chase it away. Simply set out a piece of fruit to lure it far away from you. In spite of everything, if you get stung, remove the stinger (if there is one) with tweezers, clean the skin, and apply some soothing cream.

SMALL CUTS

So you fell and your knee is bleeding. Remove the dirt and the pebbles around the edge of the wound, clean it, and apply a Band-Aid.

BRUISES AND LUMPS

Have you tripped on a branch, and now see a bruise spreading? Immediately rub some cortisone cream into the painful area so your bruise will go away more quickly.

☞ HEATSTROKE

Are you too hot and feeling ill? You probably have gotten heatstroke by staying in the sun too long. Get into the shade and drink some water or fruit juice. It will pass quickly.

☞ SMALL BURNS

Quick! Run some cold water over the burn for at least five minutes. The temperature of your skin will go down, and the burn won't go as deep into your skin. Don't put any grease on the burned spot!

☞ STINGS IN THE WATER

If you feel a sudden burning while swimming, you have been stung by a jellyfish.

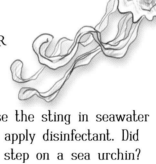

Rinse the sting in seawater and apply disinfectant. Did you step on a sea urchin? Be patient and use tweezers to pull out the spines.

If you feel a sharp pain while walking at the edge of the water, there is probably a weever fish nearby! Put your foot into very hot water to lessen the effect of the venom, which is sensitive to heat. Then clean the spot.

Courage! Little boo-boos can't keep a real adventurer down!

A FIRST AID *kit*

✳ Your first-aid kit should contain the following:
- Band-Aids
- disinfectant
- a soothing cream for insect bites
- cortisone cream
- tweezers
- cotton

Some GOOD ADVICE

✳ It's a good idea to wear beach sandals at the edge of the water.

Remember that injuries get infected more easily on dirty skin. If you don't have any disinfectant, soap and water are very helpful until an adult can take care of you.

TAKING CARE OF PLANTS WITHOUT WASTING WATER

Plants need water to grow. Here are some tricks for watering without waste!

☞ WHAT WATER?

Think about collecting rainwater for watering plants and flowers. To do that, leave a bucket or a wastebasket in your yard or on the balcony.

☞ WHEN TO WATER?

It's best to water plants early in the morning or late in the evening. Otherwise, if the sun is out and the weather is hot, you risk watering for nothing: The water will evaporate from the heat. To see if your plant needs water, poke your finger into the soil. If it comes out dry and without any soil sticking to it, water! Otherwise wait a bit.

☞ HOW TO WATER?

When you water your plants, be careful to water the base without getting water onto the leaves. When the leaves are wet, that encourages diseases that the plant could get!

☞ MULCHING

Make a little mattress so that the soil around your plant will hold its water. It can be made up of dead leaves, dead pine needles, wood chips, and so on.

That will allow the soil to hold the water, and you can water less often.

★ WHEN YOU GO ON VACATION ★

...and you are concerned about your plants, here's how to make an effective drip machine.

☞ 1 Cut the bottom off a plastic bottle.

☞ 2 Remove the cap from the bottle and plug the mouth with a piece of cotton or sponge.

☞ 3 Stick the neck of the bottle into the soil and fill the bottle with water. Your plant will get water regularly and will not suffer from your absence.

You mustn't be gone on vacation for too long.

☛ AIR OUT THE SOIL
If the soil is very dry and a little compact, scratch it up and turn it over with a rake or a hoe before watering. But be careful you don't hurt the roots! That way the water will move better.

☛ MODERATE WATERING
If you have a large pot with plants or trees in your yard, a funnel is useful in helping you avoid putting in too much water.

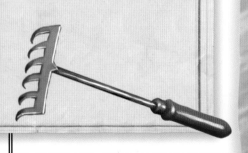

READING A MAP

Wherever he is, an adventurer is able to find his way. His best aid is a map. Here's how to read it.

⫽	Route
⸝⸝	Road
⟋	Fence
⁙	Rocky Area
⟨	Cave
⬭	Lake
∿	Brook
◯	Hill
▰	Building
▢	Isolated Tree
▭	Inhabited Area
▦	Land Under Cultivation
▭	Prairie
▭	Forest
⬭	Swamp

☛ MAP—CODED MESSAGE?
Yes! And in order to read the map correctly, you first have to know the code. Fortunately, this code is noted on every map. It is called the legend. Above all else, learn this legend. Otherwise, how will you know that a blue line represents a river, and that a green area is a forest, or that a black square marks a building?

☛ WHERE IS NORTH?

To read a map correctly, you first
have to look at it right side up. The top of the map is
the north; the bottom is south; the right is east, and the
left is west. Take your compass and place the top of
the map in the direction indicated by the needle, that
is, north. Now you know how to read the map.

What you see

☛ UP OR DOWN?

The map shows the roads and the
different types of land that you will go
through. If there is a hill, it will show
whether the hill is steep or not. So the
map tells you the layout of the land.
On a hiking map, the relief is shown by
contour lines. The closer together these
lines, the steeper the angle.

Cross-sectional
view

View from above

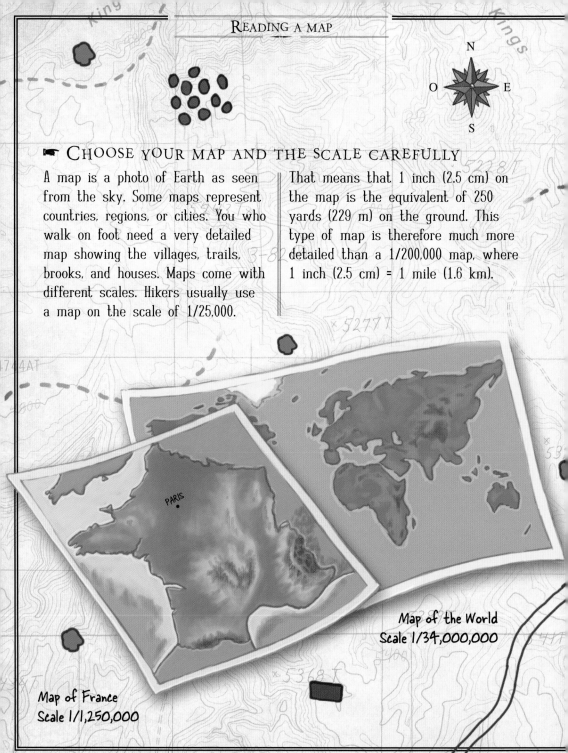

N
O · E
S

☞ CHOOSE YOUR MAP AND THE SCALE CAREFULLY

A map is a photo of Earth as seen from the sky. Some maps represent countries, regions, or cities. You who walk on foot need a very detailed map showing the villages, trails, brooks, and houses. Maps come with different scales. Hikers usually use a map on the scale of 1/25,000.

That means that 1 inch (2.5 cm) on the map is the equivalent of 250 yards (229 m) on the ground. This type of map is therefore much more detailed than a 1/200,000 map, where 1 inch (2.5 cm) = 1 mile (1.6 km).

PARIS

Map of the World
Scale 1/34,000,000

Map of France
Scale 1/1,250,000

☞ ORIENT YOUR MAP

A map is practical for finding the right route, but do you know how to locate the place where you are?
To find out, look at the surroundings. Maybe there is a forest to the right and a river to the left? Or else maybe there is a church in front of you and an agricultural field behind you? All these features are shown in the map legend.

Look for three points of reference: one to your left, one in front of you, and one on your right. Find them on the map. Set the map down flat in front of you with the identified features oriented in the right direction. Imagine lines that connect the real points in the landscape and their symbols on the map. You are located right at the spot where the lines cross!

Now you can't get lost!

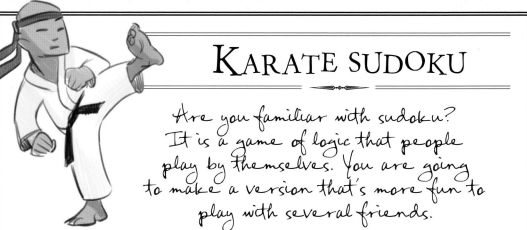

KARATE SUDOKU

*Are you familiar with sudoku?
It is a game of logic that people
play by themselves. You are going
to make a version that's more fun to
play with several friends.*

☞ THE RULES OF SUDOKU
Sudoku is a grid of six or nine boxes on a side and divided into six rectangles or nine squares. At the start of the game, certain boxes are already filled in. In order to win, you have to write in the missing numbers (from 1 to 6 or 1 to 9). Each number appears just one time on each line, in each column, and in each zone (rectangle with six boxes or square with nine boxes).

Here is one example of sudoku:

2	5			4	1
4					
5					
		2			
3					2
			3		6

And here is the solution:

2	5	3	6	4	1
4	1	6	5	2	3
5	3	1	2	6	4
6	4	2	1	3	5
3	6	5	4	1	2
1	2	4	3	5	6

MAKE YOUR OWN KARATE SUDOKU

MATERIALS
- 1 LARGE PIECE OF CARDBOARD
- 1 PAIR OF SCISSORS
- FELT-TIP MARKERS (OR COLORED PENCILS)

☞ 1

Cut out a large cardboard square. Use your felt–tip markers to draw this grid.

☞ 2

Then copy the following grid onto another piece of cardboard, color the boxes, and cut out all the game pieces.

1	1	1	1	1	1	1	1
2		2	2	2	2	2	2
3	3	3	3	3	3	3	3
4		4	4	4	4	4	4
	5	5	5	5	5	5	5
6		6	6	6	6	6	6

☞ THE RULES
FOR KARATE SUDOKU

A game for two to four players

Place the empty grid onto the table in the middle of all the players. Mix up all the numbered game pieces. Put them onto the table face down. Each player selects three game pieces and keeps them in his hand. The other game pieces make up the pool.

☞ The youngest player begins!

He puts one of his game pieces onto any box on the grid and takes a new piece from the pool. His turn is over for the moment.

☞ Then each player takes a turn putting **one of his game pieces onto one of the open boxes** on the grid, **in agreement with the rules of sudoku**: Two pieces with the same number cannot be located on the same line, in the same column, or in the same colored area (rectangle made up of six boxes).

⚠ After putting down a game piece, you always have to take a new one from the pool.

At the start of the game, it's easy:
The grid is still practically empty, and
there's no problem putting
down the pieces; but
the longer the game
goes on, the more
complicated it
becomes!

☞ **If a player cannot put
down any of his game pieces**,
he skips a turn.

How do you win?

When a player puts down the sixth
game piece on a line, a column, or
a colored area of six boxes, he
scores one point.

The game stops when the whole
grid is filled, or when nobody can
put down any more game pieces.
Then the person who has the most
points wins.

● Ready to play again? ●

THE NATIVE AMERICAN WAY

Off to the wide open spaces in the American West! You are going to learn how to be a real Native American!

Western Native Americans slept in tipis. These tents are easy to set up and to move, and they are ideal for all adventurers. Here's how to make a tipi.

● CHOOSE YOUR TIPI ●

There are various types of tipi. Choose yours based on the number and the length of the wood poles you have.

☞ NO POLES

This tipi is set up under a big horizontal, low branch, to which you attach the cloth of the tent with a strong rope. To keep everything solid, also tie the rope around the tree trunk.

☞ WITH ONE SHORT POLE

Stick the pole into the ground near a tree and tip it at an angle. This angle determines the angle of the tipi wall.

WITH ONE LONG POLE

If you have one very long pole, jam it into the fork of a tree. Set the other end at an angle on the ground.

WITH SEVERAL POLES

This is the most common type of tipi. This one doesn't need a tree to support it, but you need lots of poles to set it up.

Tie all the poles together tightly in a sort of "bouquet" and spread out the feet to form a circle on the ground.

● THE TIPI SHELL ●

The shell is a large semicircle whose radius (marked with a dotted line on the illustration) is equal to the length of the poles used for making the structure for the tent. Ask an adult to help you make some holes about every 8 inches (20 cm) all around the curved part of the material. Also make two holes in the spot that will be the top of the tipi on each side of the dotted line.

● THE FINAL SETUP ●

Spread the cloth around the poles. Thread a rope through the two holes at the top and tie this rope tightly to the top of the poles (or if you are not using poles, to the cord tied to a tree). Now all you have to do is peg the cloth to the ground with tent pegs or pieces of wood in each hole.

MAKING A BOW

1 You will need a straight flexible branch (ash, for example) that's as tall as you are.

2 Ask an adult to strip the bark off the branch with a knife.

3 If your branch is a little too thick, also ask the adult to thin it at both ends. But this is important: only on the side that will be the front of your bow. Leave the back the way it is or your bow may break.

THE BACK IS LEFT THE WAY IT IS.

THE WOOD IS THINNED ONLY ON THE FRONT SIDE

☞ **4** Ask the adult to make notches at both ends of the bow where the string will fit in. Now tie a piece of string to one end of the bow and put the string through the notch.

Before tying the string to the other end, bend the bow to give it a slightly curved shape.

◉ ARROWS ◉

Find some very straight branches. To avoid hurting anyone, ask an adult to round the tip of each arrow with a knife. You can glue some feathers onto your arrows to decorate them.

Now you are ready to be Black Eagle in a Native American adventure!

A POND IN YOUR BACKYARD

A pond attracts lots of little creatures.
You can enjoy watching them!

MATERIALS
- 1 BIG PLASTIC TARP
- SOME OLD BLANKETS
- SOME GRASS SEED
- A SHOVEL
- A PAIR OF SCISSORS

1 ☞

FIRST DIG

Dig a rounded hole at least 12 inches (30 cm) deep and about 5 feet (1.5 m) across.

☞ 2

THEN LINE IT

Put a liner on the bottom of your hole: one or more old blankets, for example.

Put a large plastic tarp over the entire surface of the pond so that it sticks out over the edges.

3 ☞
FILL IT WITH WATER

Fill your pond with water. If you have rainwater, it's better than using water from the faucet. Now all you have to do is "dress up" your pond.

☜ 4
TAKE CARE OF THE EDGES

Hide the edges of the tarp with large stones placed side by side. Cut off the tarp around the stones so only a little bit sticks out.

5

SPREAD SOME SEED

With the soil from the hole, hide the part of the tarp that sticks out. Spread some grass seed or flower seeds so that the edges of the pond quickly turn green.

6

SET UP YOUR POND

The first thing to do is to install some plants so that the little creatures feel comfortable. You can find some plants at the edge of a stream. Dig them up carefully and make sure you don't damage the roots. Plant them in small pots set on the bottom of the pond.

The water in your pond also needs to be given air. In big ponds, people install pumps that recycle the water. You can make do simply by adding water to replace the water that evaporates.

WELCOME VISITORS

The black tarp at the bottom of the pond holds in the heat.
The plants that you added quickly become food. All kinds
of creatures will come and lay eggs in the water. You can even
put in a goldfish that will eat the insect eggs and larvae.

GOOD ADVICE

IF YOU PUT IN A FISH, REMEMBER TO
FEED IT EVERY DAY UNTIL IT LEARNS
TO FIND ITS OWN FOOD. DON'T FORGET TO
STIR AROUND THE WATER REGULARLY
SO IT DOESN'T BECOME STILL!

Make a
WATER MILL

THIS IS PROBABLY ONE OF THE OLDEST MACHINES INVENTED BY HUMANS, LONG BEFORE THE WINDMILL, AROUND THE FIRST CENTURY B.C.E.!

MATERIALS

- 2 WOODEN RODS (BARBECUE SKEWERS, FOR EXAMPLE) OR 2 KNITTING NEEDLES AT LEAST 8 INCHES (20 CM) LONG
- 2 FORKED BRANCHES OF EQUAL LENGTH
- 1 CORK
- SOME SMALL, LIGHT WOOD SLATS (E.G., FROM A WOOD CRATE) (SEE THE DIMENSIONS BELOW)
- 1 CORKSCREW
- GLUE
- THE HELP OF AN ADULT IN USING A BOX CUTTER.
- A STREAM!

☛ WHAT IS IT USED FOR?

In ancient times, all difficult work was done by slaves. The first water mills, which were very powerful, were used to replace men. All they had to do was attach a mechanism to the mill's axle. That made it possible to turn a series of wheels that crushed flour, or activated a saw to cut up big wood planks, or to operate pumps.

1 ☛ Use the corkscrew to make a hole right in the center of each end of a large cork.

2 Cut six rectangles from the slats of wood to serve as the paddles. Their width needs to be the same as the length of your cork. They must be three times longer than they are wide. So if your cork is 2 inches (5 cm) long, each paddle must be 2 inches (5 cm) wide and 6 inches (15 cm) long.

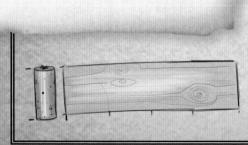

☞ **3** Ask an adult to make some perfectly straight slits from side to side, spread out around the cork. The slits need to be fairly deep, but not down to the center of the cork!

4 ☞ Glue the narrow edge of each paddle into the slits. Then let the glue dry.

☞ **5** Stick one wood rod (or 1 needle) into each hole in the ends of the cork.

☞ **6** Poke the two forked sticks into a stream, using the size of your mill to figure the distance between them.

7 ☞ Carefully place the rods of your mill into the two forks.

Look, it turns!

☞ WHAT ELSE? SOME LITTLE EXTRAS!

❊ At the ends of the sticks, you can have some fun attaching small flags that will turn along with the mill! To do this, cut two rectangles from colored paper, spread glue on the inside, and then fold them in two across each end of the sticks.

❊ You can also attach another cork to the end of one stick. If you wrap this cork with aluminum foil, it will send light signals every time the sun hits it.

❊ Finally, a little music! At the top of one of the forks, you can attach a piece of fairly large, stiff cardboard so that the paddles of the mill hit it as they turn. This will make a clicking noise.

THE MUSIC OF THE WORLD

In the evening adventurers play music around the campfire. And if they don't have any musical instruments, they make them!

★ MINI-MARACAS ★

MARACAS WERE FIRST USED BY THE NATIVE AMERICANS OF CENTRAL AMERICA. THE SOUND PRODUCED VARIES ACCORDING TO THE SIZE OF THE INSTRUMENT.

MATERIALS
- SOME SMALL YOGURT CONTAINERS
- SOME FINE GRAVEL
- GLUE
- STICKERS
- A PAIR OF SCISSORS

1 Decorate some yogurt containers (an even number) with stickers.

2 Put some gravel into one of the containers.

3 Glue a second container onto the first one to close it up.

4 Repeat the operation until you have as many maracas as you want!

Chink! Chink!
Shake your mini-maracas to the rhythm!

★ A JAPANESE DRUM ★

IN JAPAN, A DRUM IS CALLED A TAIKO.
IT MAY BE LARGE OR SMALL.

MATERIALS
- 1 EMPTY TIN CAN
- 1 BALLOON
- 1 LARGE RUBBER BAND
- 1 STICK
- 1 PIECE OF OLD CLOTH
- A PAIR OF SCISSORS
- A HAMMER

1 Ask an adult to remove the bottom from the tin can and to pound down the edges with a hammer and remove the sharp edges.

2 Then cut off the part of the balloon you blow into.

3 Stretch out the new opening so you can pull the balloon over one end of the can.

4 Hold the balloon around the can with a rubber band.

5 Is the balloon nice and tight? Make noise with your taiko by pounding on the top with a drumstick. To make a drumstick, wrap one end of a stick with a piece of cloth and make a good tight knot.

★ THE FINGER PIANO ★

IN INDONESIA, THE FINGER PIANO IS A TRADITIONAL INSTRUMENT THAT IS PLAYED DAILY FOR PLEASURE AND DURING RELIGIOUS CEREMONIES.

MATERIALS

- 1 RECTANGULAR CARDBOARD (OR METAL) BOX
- 1 LONG PIECE OF STRONG CARDBOARD 3¾ INCHES (9.5 CM) WIDE (THE LENGTH MUST BE GREATER THAN THE DEPTH OF YOUR BOX)
- SOME BIG RUBBER BANDS OF DIFFERENT WIDTHS
- A PAIR OF SCISSORS

1 ☞ Cut out a round window in the middle of your box.

2 Then cut a slit 4 inches (10 cm) long between one end of the box and the circle that you just created; make sure that there is at least ½ inch (1 cm) between each end of the slit and the edge of the box.

3 ☞ Slide the piece of cardboard vertically into this slit. It must stick up out of the slit.

4 Wrap several rubber bands around the box next to and parallel to one another; then pass them over the piece of cardboard.

5 Make the rubber bands vibrate above the hole. Rubber bands of different widths will produce different sounds depending on how tight they are.

Now it's your turn to play!

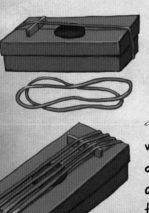

★ THE RAIN STICK ★

THIS INSTRUMENT IS COMMONLY FOUND IN AUSTRALIA AND THE SURROUNDING ISLANDS, AND ALSO IN AFRICA.

1 Use the tape to join the cardboard rolls end to end.

2 With the point of a compass, make some small holes in a spiral all around the rolls, from top to bottom. In each hole, sink a matchstick as far as possible. Make sure it doesn't go all the way through the cardboard!

MATERIALS
- 2 OR 3 EMPTY CARDBOARD ROLLS FROM PAPER TOWELS
- SOME MATCHSTICKS (OR WOODEN TOOTHPICKS)
- 1 PLASTIC BAG
- SOME RICE (OR SMALL SEEDS OR FINE GRAVEL)
- SOME TAPE
- A COMPASS

3 Cut out two squares in the plastic bag and close one end of the cylinder with one of them. Use tape to hold it in place. Don't hesitate to go around several times, because the setup has to be very solid!

4 Fill the cylinder halfway with the rice. Close the other end in the same way as the first one.

5 When you turn the rain stick end to end, the grains fall inside the cylinder and bounce off the matchsticks.

Listen carefully; you will think it's the sound of falling rain.

Make a Board Game
THE SNAIL RACE

HERE'S HOW TO MAKE AN OUTDOOR BOARD GAME!

☞ 1 THE WHEEL OF FORTUNE

It takes the place of dice! You can make it from a cheese box. From the thin cardboard, cut out a circle a little larger than the box and make this design on it.

Cut a slit along one side of the gray part. Make a cone in such a way that the gray part is hidden. Put this cone into the box.

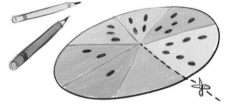

MATERIALS
- 1 PAIR OF SCISSORS
- GLUE
- FELT-TIP PENS OR PENCILS
- TAPE
- A ROUND CHEESE BOX
- THIN CARDBOARD
- A MAGAZINE
- 1 MARBLE

To play, put a marble into the box. Close it, shake it, remove the cover, and see where the marble stopped. Now you know how many boxes to move your game piece!

THE SNAIL GAME PIECES 2 ☞

Every game has to have game pieces! You need one per player.
For each game piece, cut a strip 1¼ inches (3 cm) wide from a
magazine. Roll up the strips to form cylinders: the shells.

Strengthen them using a piece of tape. For each game
piece, cut out a thin cardboard rectangle 4¾ inches
long and 1¼ inches (12 x 3 cm) wide. Cut one end
in a rounded shape to be the head.

Color each snail with a different color. Roll the
rectangles around the shells and glue them on. Leave
the heads raised. Your snail game pieces are ready!

☜ 3 THE COURSE

Trace the course for the game on the floor: Draw a
large spiral like in other board games, following this
model. Put some grass or leaves on the boxes that are
green; put some small pebbles onto the black squares; and
dig a hole for the red squares.

THE RULES

All snails are in the starting box. Each player takes a turn, starting with the
youngest. The players use a wheel of fortune and move their snails forward as
many squares as the number of points they get.

- If the snail lands on an empty square – all is well.
- On a green square: Happy to find something to eat, it moves ahead one.
- On a black square: Because it doesn't like rocks, it goes back to the starting square.
- On a red square: It falls in the hole and stays
  stuck until another snail comes
  to take its place.

**The first one to
reach the last
square wins!**

WHAT WILL THE WEATHER BE LIKE TOMORROW

Here you will find some tips for knowing if tomorrow's weather will be good enough to go off on an adventure!

☞ THE DIRECTION OF THE WIND

In most places, the wind that comes from the west sometimes brings rain. It has, in fact, passed over large bodies of water and is loaded with water vapor. Eventually, the water vapor contained in the clouds condenses; that's why it rains. So when the wind comes from the west, you may need your umbrella or raincoat.

The wind that comes from the north has passed over the North Pole and is loaded with cold air. If it's windy out, put a warm sweater into your backpack.

The wind that comes from the south has gone over warm regions. It brings dry, very warm air.

To know where the wind is coming from, the easiest thing is to make a weather vane!

★ MAKE A WEATHER VANE ★

1 Choose a shape, draw it on each piece of paper, and cut the shapes out. Many times weather vanes are in the shape of a rooster, but you can also choose any other shape.

2 Glue the two shapes together, but make sure to leave a little vertical strip without any glue from the middle to the bottom of the shape.

3 Slip a plastic cap for a pen into this space. This is what will allow your weather vane to turn freely on its axis.

4 Stick the knitting needle into the ground with the point up. You have just created the axis for the weather vane!

5 Place the cap for the pen onto the point of the axis, as if you were capping a pen. Now let the weather vane turn in the wind.

MATERIALS
- 2 SHEETS OF PAPER 8½ × 11 INCHES (22 × 28 CM)
- 1 CAP FOR A PEN
- 1 KNITTING NEEDLE
- GLUE

All you have to do is find north!

🐚 CLOUDS

There are several types of clouds. Learn to recognize them, because they will help you figure out the weather.

❄ CIRRUS

With their form that makes them look like strands, they float very high in the sky. As they are made up of ice crystals, when they arrive you can predict that the weather will change.

❄ STRATUS

Gray, flying low, and forming a thick layer, these leave no doubt about their purpose. Get ready for a day of fog and rain showers.

❄ CUMULUS

These look like big bundles of cotton or a huge pile of cotton candy. In a blue sky, they bring fair weather; you have no cause for concern.

But sometimes they cluster together and form a large mass that blocks the horizon. Then they are called cumulonimbus. In that case, get your rubber boots and your rain gear ready: You're in for a shower!

☞ RAIN

Of course, if you are on vacation, you want nice weather. And nobody really likes rain. But imagine a landscape where it never rains—a desert where nothing grows.

★ MAKE A RAIN GAUGE ★

1 ☞ Ask an adult to cut a plastic bottle in two. Turn over the top of the bottle and put it into the lower part. Your rain gauge is ready.

☞ **2** Put your rain gauge outdoors in an open area. Stick a ruler next to your bottle. Every day check the level and add up the amount of rain that has fallen.

3 ☞ By writing down the rain levels in a notebook, you can compare them from week to week. It is very interesting to note that sometimes a large storm that is violent but fast moving produces less water than a fine, steady rain. This is what the plants need in order to grow.

☛ THE SUN

The sun's light and heat are a powerful source of energy, which is captured by solar panels on the roofs of houses. Have fun measuring this energy with a radiometer.

★ MAKE A RADIOMETER ★

1
Color the dull side of the papers with a black marker.

2
Glue each piece of paper to a matchstick to make four little flags.

3
Put all the matchsticks together to make a sort of propeller and hold them together with thread.

4
Wrap this same thread around a pencil and attach it with tape.

5
Put your pencil on top of the glass jar. Put the whole thing outdoors in a sunny spot. The solar energy hits the papers; it is absorbed by the black sides and reflected by the shiny sides. The more energy there is, the quicker your propeller will spin!

YOUR HEAD IN THE STARS

The summer is the best season for looking at the stars. Not only is it warm enough to stay outdoors, but the sky is also often clear and the stars appear brighter.

☞ THE BRIGHTEST ONES

Stars are shining heavenly bodies formed by gas. There are billions and billions of them.

The easiest one to see in the daylight, and the only star in our solar system, is the sun.

Here's how to pick out some stars and constellations at night with the naked eye. To tell the difference between stars and planets, remember that stars seem to twinkle slightly, and planets are motionless. The first object you see in the evening is the planet Venus, which is also known as *the shepherd's star*. It is the brightest object. In the morning, it is in the east, and in the evening, in the west.

☛ CONSTELLATIONS

People have always enjoyed the stars and tried to recognize them.

In ancient times, scientists grouped stars together in the sky. By connecting the stars using imaginary features, they created figures: the constellations. Today, there are eighty-eight constellations that have been named! Long, long ago, the Greeks and others named them after the gods or mythological heroes, such as Orion and Andromeda.

Do you know the main constellations and their names? Here are the easiest ones to find.

✳ THE BIG DIPPER

This is the best-known constellation and the easiest one to find, with its pot shape. Once you have found the Big Dipper, look for the Little Dipper. The end of its tail is the North Star, which always shows where north is.

Little Dipper

Cassiopeia

North Star

1 2 3 4 5

Big Dipper

✳ CASSIOPEIA

Starting with the Big Dipper and passing through the Little Dipper, you arrive at Cassiopeia. Its "W" shape is easy to spot. Cassiopeia is also the name of the brightest star in this constellation.

✴ SCORPIO

The large star that shines under the head of the scorpion is Antares. In the summer, you will see only the head of the scorpion very low on the horizon. The rest of the year, you will see the whole constellation.

Scorpio in the winter

Scorpio in the summer

☞ SHOOTING STARS

Shooting stars are not really falling stars, but rather pieces of rocks or sand that burn up when they enter Earth's atmosphere. Astronomers call them *meteorites*. In the summer, generally in mid-August, we can watch "showers" of shooting stars. This results when the material from a comet touches Earth's atmosphere.

✳ THE SUMMER TRIANGLE

In the summer at night, if you look toward the south, you will see this triangle very clearly: The three stars that form it are Vega, Altair, and Deneb. Each of them belongs to a different constellation (the Lyre, the Eagle, and the Swan). This is a good starting point for finding other constellations!

Deneb

Vega

Altair

☞ THE SUMMER SKY

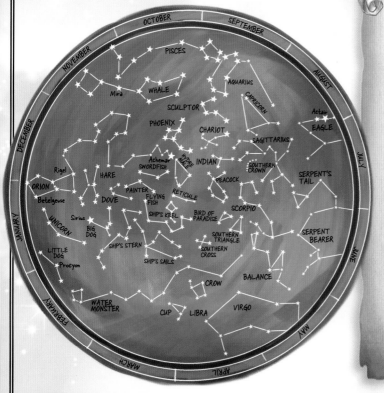

OCTOBER

SEPTEMBER

NOVEMBER

AUGUST

DECEMBER

JULY

JANUARY

JUNE

FEBRUARY

MAY

MARCH

APRIL

PISCES

AQUARIUS

CAPRICORN

Mira

WHALE

SCULPTOR

PHOENIX

CHARIOT

SAGITTARIUS

Achernar

HYDRA

INDIAN

SWORDFISH

MALE

Altair

EAGLE

SOUTHERN

CROWN

SERPENT'S

TAIL

Rigel

HARE

PEACOCK

ORION

PAINTER

RETICULE

Betelgeuse

DOVE

FLYING

FISH

SCORPIO

Sirius

SHIP'S KEEL

BIRD OF

PARADISE

SERPENT

BEARER

UNICORN

BIG

DOG

SOUTHERN

TRIANGLE

LITTLE

DOG

SHIP'S STERN

SOUTHERN

CROSS

Procyon

SHIP'S SAILS

BALANCE

CROW

WATER

MONSTER

CUP

LIBRA

VIRGO

☞ DO STARS MOVE?

Like the moon, the stars appear to move across the sky during the night.
Of course, this is because Earth turns! This explains why certain stars can only be seen at certain times of the year, and why the sky maps you see in books are dated with a season—summer or winter!

RACES ON THE WATER

If your adventures take you to the edge of the water, take advantage of it to organize some boat races!

★ A MOTOR BOAT ★

YOU CAN MAKE YOUR MOTORBOAT FROM A PIECE OF BOARD OR BARK. THE MOTOR IS MADE FROM A PROPELLER AND A RUBBER BAND.

THE HULL

1 ☞

If you use a piece of thin board, ask an adult to make it bigger and reproduce this shape on the board, and then to cut it out. Your boat should measure a little more than 4 inches (10 cm) wide and 6–8 inches (15–20 cm) long.

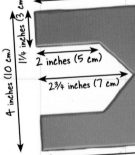

4 inches (10 cm)

1¼ inches (3 cm)

4 inches (10 cm)

2 inches (5 cm)

2¾ inches (7 cm)

6 inches (15 cm)

Or you may also find a piece of tree bark. For example, sometimes you can pick up large pieces of bark under pines and fir trees. Bark is not as hard as wood, and you can easily shape it like a boat. The best of all is cork, which floats very well and will almost never sink!

THE MOTOR AND PROPELLER

MATERIALS
- SEVERAL SMALL WOOD RECTANGLES
- 1 RUBBER BAND

1 First attach the rubber band to the two parts that stick out the back of the boat.

2 Slip a rectangle of wood into the middle of the two rear parts, between the two lengths of rubber band.

3 Wind up this little strip (it becomes the propeller for your boat). The rubber band gets twisted. Hold it firmly until the start of the race.

THE RACE

Has everyone now made a boat and wound up the rubber band as tight as it will go? Now carefully set your boat on the surface of the water, and—One! Two! Three! Let go! The rubber band unwinds at top speed! The propeller turns, and the boat moves forward!

Who will win the race?

★ A SAILBOAT ★

FLEETS OF SHIPS ARE RACING. THEY HEAD OUT TO DISCOVER DISTANT, MYSTERIOUS COUNTRIES. WHICH FLEET WILL BE THE FIRST ONE TO REACH LAND?

Make a whole fleet of mini-sailing ships with walnut shells.

MATERIALS
- WALNUT SHELLS
- I SHEET OF CARDSTOCK
- SHEET OF PAPER
- SOME TOOTHPICKS
- I PENCIL
- A PAIR OF SCISSORS

1 ☞ Choose some half shells without any cracks or holes.

☜ **2** Turn your shells over on the cardstock. Trace around them.

3 ☞ Cut out these shapes.

4 Place them into the half shells to "plug" them.

5 ☞ Stick a toothpick into each piece of cardstock.

6 Cut out some small squares of paper to act as sails.

7 ☞ Decorate them with the colors of your fleet. Stick a sail onto each toothpick.

THE OCEAN RACE

With your friends, decide on a destination for your route. That will be the "unknown land" to be discovered. Put all your little boats into the water. Each captain must move his boats along by blowing on the sails.

Which great ocean adventurer will be the first to reach the destination?

MAKE AN HERBARIUM

Gather some flowers and plants
to make an herbarium and
become a botanical pro!

❦ STEP ONE: GATHERING ✿

Take a small notebook to
jot down your notes, and
a bag for gathering the plants.

The Best Time for Gathering

The middle of the day, because
then the plants are not covered
with dew. Collect just one example
of each species, and before
collecting it, make sure that it
is whole and in good condition:
The stem, the leaves, and the
petals must not be damaged.

✦ STEP TWO: DRYING ✦

MATERIALS

- I NEWSPAPER (OR PAPER TOWEL)
- SOME CARDBOARD
- SHEETS OF PAPER 8½ INCHES × II INCHES (22 × 28 CM)
- SOME PIECES OF BOARD
- SOME WOOD SKEWERS
- A PAIR OF SCISSORS
- TAPE

IN ORDER TO PRESERVE FLOWERS CORRECTLY, THEY MUST BE FREE OF ANY TRACE OF WATER.

1 Place each example between two pieces of newspaper (or paper towel). Be sure to flatten all parts of the plant.

2 To keep the flowers from "sweating" onto one another, place a piece of cardboard between the pieces of newspaper that contain a flower.

3 Place the pile thus formed between the boards and put something heavy on top, such as a dictionary or a big rock.

Let your plants dry for ten days.

❀ STEP THREE: THE HERBARIUM ❀

☞ **1** Fold the sheets of paper in two (as many sheets as plants). Along this fold, cut seven notches about ³⁄₈ inch (1 cm) deep, regularly spread along the length.

2 ☞

Place two sheets together, one facing right and the other left, by overlapping the notches.

☞ **3** Attach them together.

To do that, slide a wood skewer into the lower fold of sheet number one so it comes out of the first notch of this same sheet. Then pass it into the first notch of sheet number two and have it come out at the second notch of this same sheet. Next pass it into the second notch of sheet number one, and have it come out at the third notch of this same sheet.

Continue all the way to the top.

#3

👉 4

It's easy to add an extra sheet!
Turn your herbarium over and press
down all the unused notches of sheet
number one. Take a new notched sheet and
another skewer. Insert the skewer into the
fold at the bottom of sheet number one
and continue in the same way as before.

Using this method, your herbarium can expand
along with the results of your gathering.

❀ STEP 4: TAPING 🌱

Are the collected plants nice and dry? Gently place them
onto each page of your herbarium. A bit of tape to hold
them in place, and you are ready to go!

Then you can write next to each plant the place
and the date you collected it.

With a little
research, you
will surely find
out what they
are called.

THE MYSTERY OF CHERRIES

A little summer puzzle to free up some cherries. Serious thought guaranteed!

👉 1 Cut out a large shape of a cherry leaf from the green plastic.

MATERIALS
- 1 PIECE OF FLEXIBLE GREEN PLASTIC (OR ELSE A PIECE OF LEATHER)
- 2 CHERRIES ATTACHED TO ONE ANOTHER
- A PAIR OF SCISSORS

🍒 THE LEAF

Leaf

Split

Hole

👉 2 Cut two slits and a hole as shown in the picture.

🍒 THE PUZZLE

Attention: Here is the secret of the puzzle! Practice several times so you can lock in the cherries quickly and easily.

1 👉 Fold the leaf in half.

2 👉 Stick the thin central strip through the hole.

3 👉 Pull on the strip so it makes a loop large enough to slip one of the cherries through.

4 👉 Flatten out the leaf again: The central strip goes back into place and locks in the cherries!

🍒 MYSTIFY YOUR FRIENDS!

Now that you know how to lock in the cherries, you can also release them. Slide the central strip into the hole, make a large loop, and pass one of the cherries through it! Easy! Your friends who don't know the secret will have a hard time figuring this out!

THE ADVENTURER'S POUCH

Make a pouch for hiding some coins and your little treasures!

1 Put the plate upside down onto your piece of cloth. The plate must fit inside the edges.

2 Trace around it. This will give you a nice round circle.

Cut out the circle. **3**

MATERIALS
- 1 LARGE PIECE OF THICK CLOTH (OR THIN BUT STRONG PLASTIC)
- 2 STRINGS
- A PLATE
- A PEN
- A PAIR OF POINTED SCISSORS

4 With the point of your scissors, punch sixteen holes spaced out evenly along the inner edge of the circle.

5 Thread a string into all the holes, switching above and below the cloth.

6 Count eight holes from the starting point. Starting with the eighth hole, thread in the second string the same way as the first one.

You can even tie it to your belt, just like Robin Hood did!

7 Pull on the two strings, and your pouch will close!

How to catch fish

Adventurers sometimes have to find their own food. When you are near water, fishing is a good way to get food.

★ WATCHING FISH ★

BEFORE FISHING, YOU FIRST HAVE TO KNOW IF THERE ARE ANY FISH WHERE YOU ARE. BUT IT'S HARD TO SEE THROUGH THE WATER BECAUSE LIGHT COMES OFF THE SURFACE. IT KEEPS YOU FROM SEEING WHAT IS GOING ON BELOW. BUT RELAX! HERE IS A WAY TO SPY ON THE FISH.

1 Ask an adult to cut the top and the bottom off a large plastic bottle.

MATERIALS
- 1 PLASTIC BOTTLE
- PLASTIC WRAP FROM THE KITCHEN
- 1 RUBBER BAND (OR STRING)
- A PAIR OF SCISSORS

2 Put some plastic wrap onto one end of the bottle and hold it tightly in place with the rubber band or string.

3 To look deep into the water, stick the part of the bottle covered by plastic wrap below the surface, and you will be surprised to see very clearly everything that's going on!

★ MAKE A FISHING ROD ★

NOW THAT YOU HAVE FOUND A SPOT WHERE THERE ARE SOME FISH, ALL YOU HAVE TO DO IS CATCH THEM.

1 Find a straight, flexible tree branch— a branch from an ash tree, for example. Careful! Don't just break off this branch. Ask an adult to cut it off correctly without harming the tree.

MATERIALS
- 1 LONG, FLEXIBLE TREE BRANCH
- 6 FEET (2 M) OF THREAD (OR STRING)
- 1 CORK
- 1 MATCHSTICK
- MODELING CLAY
- 1 PAPER CLIP
- A KNIFE

2 Tie the line to the thin end of the branch. It's best to find a length of nylon line like real fishermen use; but, if you don't have any, a cotton thread or thin string will work fine.

3
Make a hole through the middle of the cork.

4
Slide the cork on about 20 inches (50 cm) from the end of the line. To keep it in place, force a matchstick into the hole.

5
About 8 inches (20 cm) from the end of the line, attach a little ball of modeling clay around the line. This will weight down the hook and keep the line from floating. The cork will serve as the "bobber" for the fishing rod.

6
Tie your hook to the end of the line.
Use the paper clip to make a little pointed hook.

★ HOW TO FISH ★

1
First of all, put some bait onto your hook. You can look for earthworms that hide in the soil under the damp leaves, or use a little ball of bread, a kernel of wheat, or a tiny piece of cheese.

☞ **2** Now toss your line into the water.

3 ☜

Finally, make yourself comfortable at the edge of the water (sometimes you have to wait a long time for a fish to bite the hook).

☞ **4** The ball of modeling clay helps your hook sink in the water. The bobber stays on the surface. This is what you have to watch: If a fish bites the bait, it will pull on the line and the bobber will dip into the water. At this instant, you raise your pole quickly and catch the fish!

5 ☞

If you don't want to eat the fish, or it is too little, carefully remove the hook and quickly put the fish back into the water.

Good luck!

BIRD-WATCHING

To attract birds you can put seeds out on the windowsill.

THE WINTER IS THE BEST TIME TO MAKE A BIRD FEEDER BECAUSE IT'S HARD FOR THE BIRDS TO FIND FOOD.

1 ☞ Ask an adult to cut the top off the first bottle. Keep only the part with the neck.

MATERIALS
- 2 PLASTIC BOTTLES
- A STICK ABOUT 8 INCHES (20 CM) LONG AND 3/8 OF AN INCH (1 CM) IN DIAMETER
- 12 INCHES (30 CM) OF STRING
- BIRDSEED
- A PERMANENT MARKER
- A PAIR OF SCISSORS
- A BOX CUTTER

2 Have the adult cut off the bottom of the second bottle. This time keep both parts.

3 ☞ On the first bottle, draw two windows on opposite sides.

Ask an adult to cut out the windows with the box cutter.

4 ☞ Put the second bottle upside down into the first one.

☞ 5 Make two holes under each opening and slide the stick through. It will serve as a perch.

6 ☞ Make two more holes on top for attaching the string. It will be used to hang up the feeder.

☞ 7 Pour some seeds into the upside-down bottle. They will fall down through the neck. Put the bottom of the second bottle on top of the feeder and put in some water.

☞ 8 Set up your feeder at least 5 feet (1.5 m) off the ground so that the birds will not be bothered by cats or other predators.

☞ 9 Don't forget to clean the feeder regularly!

The best time of the year for feeding your feathered friends is between early November and the end of March. What kind of food? Birds really like sunflower seeds. And in the dead of winter, pieces of fat will give them the necessary energy for flying. Chickadees, finches, robins, and sparrows also like cooked rice. If you have any leftovers from dinner, you can give them a treat!

Close-ups of some birds

Here are the main visitors that may come to take advantage of your feeder.

🐦 ROBIN

Robins are small, 5½ inches (14 cm), and easily recognizable with their red-orange breasts and darker backs.

Robins like the woods and mixed vegetation, and they fly from one perch to another not far above the ground.

🐦 COMMON BLACKBIRD

The common blackbird is all black with a yellow beak. It lives in the woods, the underbrush, parks, and yards. It searches for insects and earthworms; this is why it usually flies low.

🐦 CROW

The crow is larger than the blackbird—about 18 inches (45 cm). It, too, is all black, including its beak! One distinguishing feature: the end of its tail is square. Crows are very partial to seedlings in fields, but they are also scavengers (they eat dead animals). Some crows have a lighter-colored beak.

CHICKADEE

The chickadee has some color! The feathers on the head, wings, and tail are dark, and the belly is yellow. Chickadees like deciduous forests (woods with trees that lose their leaves in the winter) and take shelter in hollows and holes in trees.

MAGPIE

A magpie is easy to recognize because of its colors—black (beak) and white (stomach)—and because of its long tail and large size 18-24 inches (45-60 cm). It lives in fairly open or lightly wooded spaces and on grasslands. If you ever see a bird perched on a sheep, there's a good chance it's a magpie!

WAGTAIL

White, gray, and black, a wagtail catches insects on the ground or in flight. It likes to live near water, ponds, pools, and in fairly open places such as fields or the edges of roads.

NIGHTINGALE

The nightingale, with its brown and light beige color, blends into the landscape. The nightingale likes the woods and thick underbrush, and often stays on the ground or in the bushes. The nightingale sings during the day and also at night.

SAILORS' KNOTS

There are a number of sailors' knots. Get a couple of short lengths of rope and practice tying them!

FOLLOW THE INSTRUCTIONS IF YOU NEED TO TIE UP A BOAT, GO CLIMBING, TIE SOME THINGS DOWN, OR HANG ONTO SOMETHING!

BOWLINE (1 ROPE)

THIS IS A STRONG KNOT THAT IS STILL EASY TO UNTIE! TO REMEMBER HOW TO TIE IT, THINK OF THE SENTENCE, "I COME OUT OF THE WELL, GO AROUND THE TREE, AND GO BACK DOWN INTO THE WELL."

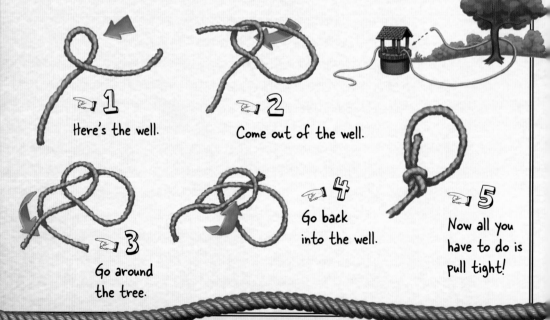

1 Here's the well.

2 Come out of the well.

3 Go around the tree.

4 Go back into the well.

5 Now all you have to do is pull tight!

FISHERMAN'S BEND (1 ROPE)

THE FISHERMAN'S BEND IS USED FOR ATTACHING A ROPE
TO A RING OR AN OBJECT TO KEEP IT FROM SLIDING.
CAREFUL: ONCE IT'S TIGHT, IT IS DIFFICULT TO UNTIE!

☞ **1** First make a
round turn.

☞ **2** Pass the short
end through
the two loops
formed by the
round turn.

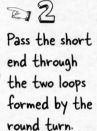

☞ **3** Now make the
first half hitch
as shown.

☞ **4** Now make a
second one
in the same
direction.

☞ **5** Pull tight
to keep everything
together.

OVERHAND KNOT (1 ROPE)

THIS IS ONE OF THE STRONGEST KNOTS, AND IT IS VERY USEFUL
FOR KEEPING AN ITEM FROM SLIPPING! BUT IT IS NOT ALWAYS
EASY TO UNTIE. IT IS ALSO CALLED THE FIGURE-EIGHT KNOT.

1 ☞ Make a
loop.

2 ☞ Go under
the rope.

3 ☞ Then go into the loop
from the top.

☞ **4** Pull tight!

SQUARE KNOT (2 ROPES)

THIS IS AN EASY KNOT TO TIE. IT CAN BE USED TO TIE TWO ROPES TOGETHER OR FOR TYING LACES.

1 👉 Make a first half hitch with the ends of two different ropes.

2 👉 Next, make another half hitch but in the other direction.

3 👉 Tighten and check the strength of the knot.

GOT IT? NOW YOU ARE KING OF THE SAILORS' KNOTS, SO MAYBE YOU WANT TO DEMONSTRATE FOR A REAL SAILOR. BUT CAREFUL! THERE ARE CERTAIN WORDS YOU MUST NOT SAY AND CERTAIN THINGS YOU MUST NOT DO ABOARD AN OLD CAPTAIN'S SHIP.

👉 ROPE
Don't say this word!
Use the word *line*.
String is also avoided.

☞ A RAINBOW AT SEA

If you see a rainbow at sea, don't point at it! People say that could attract a storm.

☞ THE RABBIT

You will hear sailors speak of this animal using the expression "the long-eared creature." Long ago, when a rabbit got onto a boat, it nibbled on the ropes and the wood. The little animal thus nearly made the whole ship go down!

☞ WHISTLING

Shhh! The only one who can whistle aboard a ship is the cook. In fact, as long as the cook is whistling, he is not eating the sailors' food!

ANIMAL TRACKS

Turn yourself into a detective adventurer and follow animals by their tracks!

🐾 FOOTPRINTS 🐾

NEAR A MUDDY TRAIL, AROUND A POND, ON A SNOWY ROAD, OR IN SLIGHTLY MOIST SAND, LOOK FOR ANIMAL TRACKS. ONCE YOU SPOT THEM, USE THE FOLLOWING DRAWINGS TO FIGURE OUT WHO THEY BELONG TO!

Large Tracks

| Horse | Cow | Goat | Deer | Sheep | Wild Boar |

Medium Tracks

| Dog | Cat | Fox | Badger |

Small Tracks

Front feet

Rear feet

| Hedgehog | Squirrel | Mink | Rabbit | Hare | Mouse | Rat |

Birds

| Duck | Owl | Pheasant | Gull | Sparrow | Seagull | Goose | Magpie | Pigeon |

◖ MORE SIGNS ❁

THERE ARE ALSO OTHER TYPES OF SIGNS YOU CAN TRY TO FOLLOW.

☛ FEATHERS AND HAIRS

A feather on the ground—is it black and white like a magpie feather, or full of color like a peacock feather? Hairs caught on a fence—are they from a sheep, a dog, or a cow?

☛ DENS AND LAIRS

A hole in an embankment—check the size. Maybe it's the entrance to a den of rats or skunks, 2½-3½ inches (6-9 cm), or rabbits, 4-6 inches (10-15 cm), or even foxes, 6-10 inches (15-25 cm).

☛ DROPPINGS

Little round droppings on the grass show that a rabbit has been in the area.

If the droppings are thin, long, and brown, they are probably from a hedgehog.

And in the woods, acorn-shaped droppings stuck together are from a deer.

☞ SIGNS YOU CAN SMELL

Do you smell cheese? There is a billy goat somewhere around.

Is there a broken eggshell on the ground? Surely a marten has been through the area.

⚠ ★ SHHH! ★

You have to be unnoticeable when watching animals. Before setting out, put on gray or green clothing.

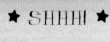

If you listen carefully, you will hear a thousand little sounds that you have never before paid attention to. Take along a pair of binoculars, be patient, and sit near a watering hole. With a little luck, you will see lots of animals.

❨ A WILD BOAR'S TRAIL ❨

The wild boar is an animal that leaves easily recognizable signs.

It lives in the woods and the forests with water sources (ponds and rivers). During the day, it rests among the bushes, and, in the early evening, it becomes very active. Wild boars like to rub against oak trees and eat the acorns. So if you see an oak tree, look carefully beneath it.

Are there black droppings (stuck together in the winter and spread around in the summer)? Hairs? Or traces of mud on the trunk? Chewed, half-crushed acorns are another sign.

The wild boar is also a burrower: It scratches up the ground. So if you see a section of ground churned up or leaves that have been moved around, you can be sure that a wild boar has passed through.

GOOD ADVICE

Wild boars have poor eyesight, but they have very good noses and excellent hearing. Wild boars often live in bands, and the female, the sow, can be dangerous if she believes that someone is coming too close to her young. So be careful. An adventurer needs to keep a sharp eye out and stay away from wild animals!

Keep on the right track!

A GARDEN

Making your own garden is a good way to have fresh vegetables for your picnics!

★ PLANT SOME CHERRY TOMATOES

AS YOU START YOUR CAREER AS A GARDENER, CHOOSE CHERRY TOMATOES. THEY ARE EASY TO TAKE CARE OF, GROW QUICKLY, AND TASTE DELICIOUS!

MATERIALS
- CHERRY TOMATO PLANTS
- SOME STICKS (STAKES) AT LEAST 20 INCHES (50 CM) LONG
- STRING
- A SHOVEL

1 You can find cherry tomato plants at any garden supplies store in the spring.

2 Choose a sunny spot and dig a large hole 8 inches (20 cm) deep for each little plant.

3 Put a stake into each hole.

☞ **4** Put a plant into each hole in such a way that it touches the stake. Now fill the hole back up with the soil and stamp it down with your fists.

5 ☞

Remember to water your tomato plants every day, in the evening so that the heat doesn't evaporate all the water. The plants will grow very quickly.

☞ **6**

Carefully tie the plants to the stakes with string.

7 ☞

Starting in July (and maybe even sooner), you will be able to harvest delicious cherry tomatoes every day. Pluck them carefully. Grasp the stem of the tomato between your fingers and break it off cleanly, and be careful to avoid damaging the plant.

Enjoy!

★ KEEPING THE BIRDS AWAY ◉

Birds also like to eat cherry tomatoes!
To keep the birds from stealing them,
you need to scare the birds away.
A good scarecrow will do the trick!

MATERIALS

- STRAW
- 2 LONG WOOD POLES
- SOME OLD CLOTHING:
- 1 PAIR OF PANTS, 1 T-SHIRT, AND 1 SHIRT
- A CLOTH BAG
- SOME WOOD STAKES (BARBECUE SKEWERS)
- ALUMINUM FOIL
- SOME CORD
- LARGE MARKERS
- SOME OLD CDS
- A PAIR OF SCISSORS

☞ THE BODY

1 ☞ Put one leg of the pants onto the longer pole. Stick the pole into the ground.

☞ 2 Fill the pants with straw so that they stand up by themselves.

3 Put the T-shirt over the top of the pole. Then slide the second pole through the two sleeves.

☞ 4 Tie the second pole to the first one with the cord to form a cross. Fill the T-shirt with straw.

5 ☞ Put the shirt over the T-shirt and stuff some more straw into the sleeves to solidify the top.

The body is done!

☞ THE HEAD

☞ 1 Using the large markers, draw the eyes, the mouth, and the nose of your scarecrow onto the front of your bag. The bottom of the face is near the opening of the bag.

2 ☞ Fill the bag with straw, then use the cord to close it—but don't pull it tight.

3 ☞ Slide the bag onto the vertical pole and tie the knot tight to attach the head to the body.

☞ THE FINISHING TOUCHES

☞ 1 Make some hair by cutting out long strips of aluminum foil. Stick these to the head with the wood skewers. They will move with the wind, and the flashes of light will frighten away birds.

2 ☞ You can also tie some strings to the hands of the scarecrow and hang the CDs. The wind will make them spin and they will flash in the light.

So long, you greedy birds!

115

SEND NEWS!

Send a card to your friends and tell them what you are up to! What could be better than personalizing them by making them yourself?

NO NEED TO BUY A SIMPLE POSTCARD! YOU CAN MAKE A 3-D CARD AND THE ENVELOPE TO GO WITH IT!

★ THE 3-D CARD ◑

MATERIALS
- 2 8½ × 11 INCHES (22 × 28 CM) SHEETS OF CARD STOCK IN DIFFERENT COLORS
- VARIOUS SMALL LEAVES
- GLUE
- A PAIR OF SCISSORS
- PHOTO
- PEN

1 ☞ Fold the sheets of card stock in half.

2 ☞ Cut a strip ¾ inch (2 cm) wide from the length of each sheet. Careful: Don't cut the side where the fold is!

¾ inch (2 cm)

1½ inches (4 cm)

1½ inches (4 cm)

3 ☞ Set one of these two sheets aside. Cut some slits about 1½ inches (4 cm) deep along the fold of the other one.

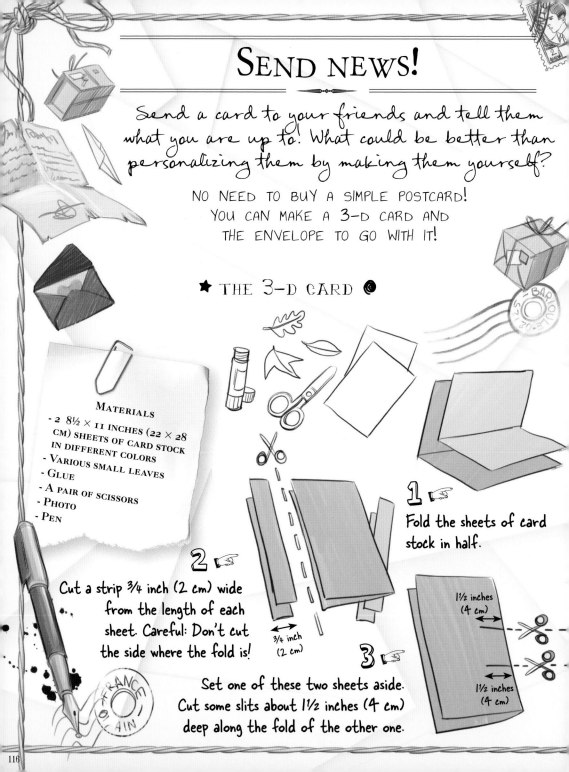

☞ **4** Fold up the parts near the ends of the card and make a fold.

☞ **5** Open up the card and make two "steps."

6 ☞ Close the card back up and once again make a cut in the center of each step.

7 ☞ Open once again and form the "stairs."

☞ **8** Take the first piece of card stock and glue it to the back of the one that you cut out.

9 ☞ Now glue the leaves vertically to each step to create a forest landscape.

10 Finally, glue your photo among the trees. Write a little message on your card in front of the scene that you have just created.

Your card is all done!

★ A CUSTOM ENVELOPE ◉

MATERIALS
- SHEET OF WHITE 12 × 16 INCHES (30 × 40 CM) PAPER
- 1 STAMP
- A PEN
- A PAIR OF SCISSORS

1
Put your folded 3-D card diagonally in the center of the sheet. Trace around it.

2
Make a fold along the short side by folding the paper over your card.

3
Do the same thing with the other short side.

4 👉

Now fold along one of the long sides, carefully lining up the left and right edges. Slip your card into the envelope.

👉 **5**

Finish up by folding along the last long side, again being careful to line up the edges.

👉 **6**

Turn your envelope over.

👉 **7**

Now all you have to do is fold over the little corner that sticks out and hold it in place with a stamp!

8 👉

Write the address, put your card into a mailbox, and soon your friends will know what you are up to—and they will get a nice little present!

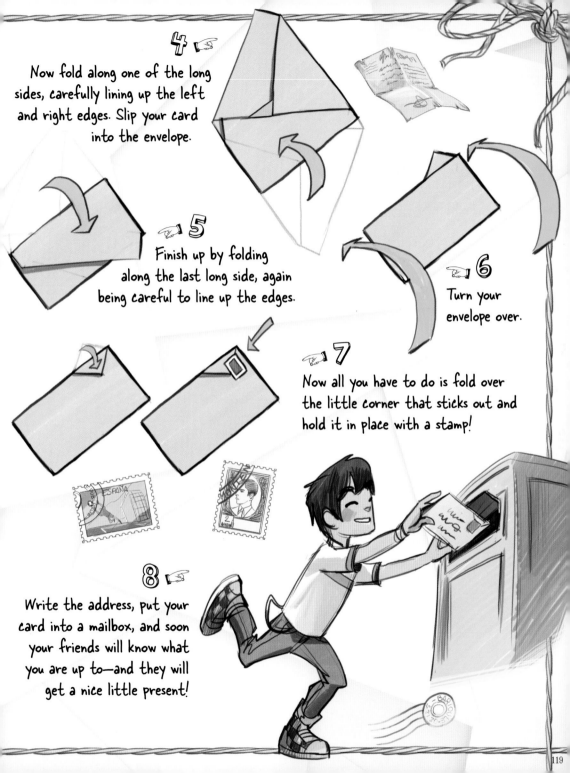

THE MARTIAN

MAKE A LITTLE GREEN-HEADED MAN
WITH HAIR THAT REALLY GROWS!

MATERIALS

- 1 STOCKING OR THIN SOCK
- GRASS SEED
- SOME WOOD SHAVINGS
  OR SAND
- 2 YOGURT CONTAINERS
- GLUE
- PERMANENT MARKERS
- SOME STICKERS

1 Put a small handful of grass seed into the toe of the stocking. On top of this, add a handful of wood shavings. When you think you have enough, make a ball and tie it up to hold everything inside. This is the Martian's head!

2 Make the body by gluing the yogurt containers together. This stack forms the body. Use the markers and the stickers to decorate your Martian. Stick the head into the top container.

3 Put your Martian into a sunny place and water it every day. In less than a week, your little guy will have green hair growing on his head!

REMOVING THE SALT FROM SEAWATER

Here's a hint for turning saltwater into fresh!

1 Dig a hole in the ground and put the container inside it.

2 Put the plastic over the hole. Keep it in place with one large stone on each side to keep it from falling into the hole. Put the smallest stone in the center of the plastic to make it concave.

3 Pour some saltwater into the hole. Make sure you don't get any inside the container!

4 Now let the sun do its work. With the heat, the saltwater will evaporate and condense in fine droplets.

Because you put a stone in the middle of the plastic, the drops will run down to the lowest point and collect. When they are big enough, they will fall into the container. The water evaporates, but the salt that it contains stays on the soil.

So you will have the pleasant surprise of drinking pure water!